insight text guide

Russell Smith

The Curious Incident of the Dog in the Night-time

Mark Haddon

First published in 2004, reprinted in 2007, 2009, 2011, 2014, 2015 (twice), 2018, 2019, 2020 (twice), 2021, 2022, 2024.

Insight Publications Pty Ltd
3/350 Charman Road
Cheltenham VIC 3192
Australia
Tel: +61 3 8571 4950
Email: books@insightpublications.com.au

www.insightpublications.com.au

National Library of Australia Cataloguing-in-Publication entry:
Smith, Russell Brian.
Insight text guide: The curious incident of the dog in the night-time, Mark Haddon.
For senior secondary English students.
ISBN 9781920693619
1. Haddon, Mark.—Criticism and interpretation. 2. Haddon, Mark. The curious incident of the dog in the night-time. I. Title.
(Series: Insight text guide).
823.914

Other ISBNs:
9781922378606 (digital)

Cover design: The Modern Art Production Group

Printed by Markono Print Media Pte Ltd

contents

CHARACTER MAP

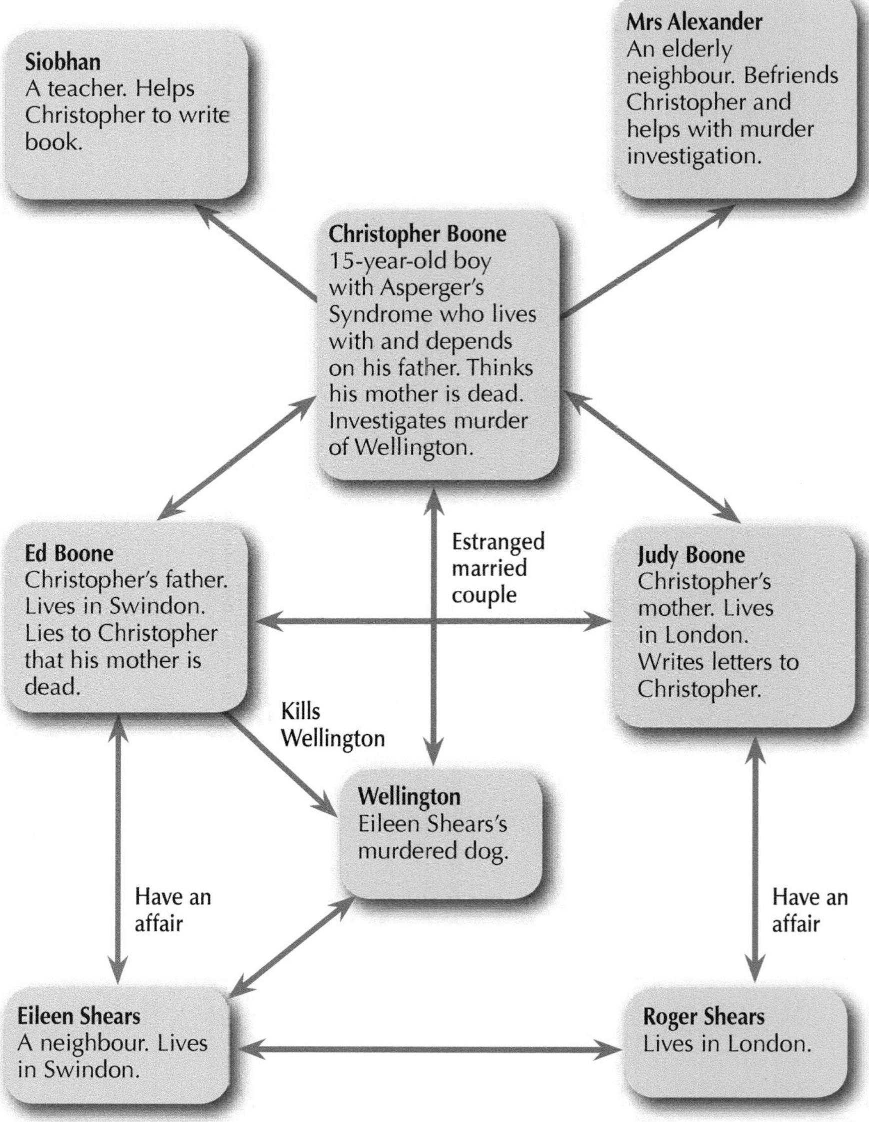

INTRODUCTION

Fifteen-year-old Christopher Boone is one of the most unusual narrators in modern fiction.

He has a photographic memory, is brilliant at solving puzzles and can do complex mathematical problems in his head. But he also has some odd habits: he won't eat foods that are touching on the plate, avoids anything coloured yellow or brown, and believes that if he sees five red cars in a row it will be a 'Super Good Day' (p.31).

Christopher has Asperger's Syndrome, a mild form of autism, which means that he feels no emotional connection with other people, even his parents. He prefers to be alone, hates being touched, and finds people confusing because he cannot understand their facial expressions. He avoids strangers and crowds, and has never been further than the end of the street on his own. If he gets frightened or confused he will lash out violently or curl up in a ball and make the sound his father calls 'groaning': 'I make this noise when there is too much information coming into my head from the outside world' (p.8).

But if Christopher finds people confusing, he loves dogs, because they only have four moods, 'happy, sad, cross and concentrating', and because 'dogs are faithful and they do not tell lies because they cannot talk' (p.4). Therefore, when Christopher discovers that someone has killed his neighbour's dog with a garden fork, he decides to investigate the murder. In the course of his investigation Christopher makes the shocking discovery that his father has lied to him about his mother being dead, and he sets out on a terrifying journey to be reunited with her.

Mark Haddon's novel is a brilliant feat of the imagination, an attempt to get inside the thoughts and emotions of someone who in real life would probably not be interested in communicating with us in such a moving and entertaining fashion. A successful author of children's books, Haddon worked earlier in his life as a carer for people with behavioural problems and drew on this experience in creating Christopher Boone.

The novel works on many levels: it's a poignant story of a dysfunctional family struggling to cope with Christopher's behavioural problems, a portrait of a loving father who battles to regain his son's trust, and an inspiring adventure in which Christopher's courage and determination are tested to the limit. Along the way the novel also explores philosophical questions about emotion, personality, and the nature of language, where it seems it is often easier to lie than to tell the truth.

But what's best about the novel is Christopher's engaging way of telling his story, which is interspersed with maps, diagrams and puzzles, and entertaining digressions on his favourite subjects, from the Milky Way galaxy and the theory of relativity to the famous Monty Hall Problem.

Note: Because of its awkward title, the novel will be referred to by the short title *The Curious Incident...*.

BACKGROUND & CONTEXT

About the Author

When he published *The Curious Incident...*, Mark Haddon was already the author of fifteen books of children's fiction. He graduated in English from Merton College, Oxford, in 1981, and worked for several years as a volunteer carer for adults and children with behavioural problems and physical disabilities. He drew on this experience for some aspects of the characterisation of Christopher Boone. He also worked as a cartoonist and illustrator before turning to writing children's books, all of which he illustrated himself. In his spare time he enjoys painting and looking after his two young children.

The Novel's Reception

Echoing the Harry Potter phenomenon, *The Curious Incident...* is a rare example of a book published simultaneously in a children's edition (David Fickling Books) and an adults' edition (Random House). It was an instant critical and commercial success. There was controversy in September 2003, when the chairman of the judging panel for the prestigious Man Booker Prize, John Carey, criticised his fellow judges for not including it on their shortlist.[1] This omission perhaps reflects a prejudice that children's books cannot simultaneously be regarded as serious adult fiction. However, as well as the *Guardian* Children's Fiction Prize in 2003, *The Curious Incident...* won the prestigious Whitbread Book of the Year Prize in 2004. It has since been published in 32 countries in 15 different languages, and will be made into a feature film by the production company that made the Harry Potter films.

[1] John Ezard, 'Curious incident of writer's literary hat trick', *Guardian*. 13 November 2003.

Notes on Asperger's Syndrome

Although he doesn't refer to it by its medical name anywhere in his story, Christopher Boone has a condition known as Asperger's Syndrome, a mild form of autism. Much of the medical information here is taken from an article by Peter Szatmari.[2] Before you read this section, however, bear in mind that Christopher Boone is not intended to be a medical 'case study'. Mark Haddon is often asked by readers whether he did specific research into Asperger's Syndrome before he wrote the novel. Here is what he writes in reply:

> I did no specific research at all. Many years ago I worked with people with a variety of disabilities (all of them more seriously disabled than Christopher) so I feel comfortable writing about the subject and have what you might call an interested layperson's knowledge of autism and Asperger's. Beyond that I reasoned...that the novel would work best if I simply tried to make Christopher seem like a believable human being, rather than trying to make him medically 'correct'.[3]

Asperger's Syndrome is sometimes called High Functioning Autism. Autism is a developmental condition in which children have difficulties interacting emotionally with other people, even with their parents. Although often highly intelligent, autistic children find it difficult to interpret the ordinary 'cues' of emotional interaction that most people respond to almost automatically, such as inflections of the voice, physical gestures and facial expressions. They appear to live in an 'inner world' of their own, and often need a familiar, highly structured environment in order to feel safe. These difficulties extend into adulthood and old age, and severely autistic people often live either part-time or full-time in institutions. Some autistic people, popularly known as 'autistic savants', demonstrate amazing capabilities in specific intellectual tasks, such as having a photographic memory or performing complex mathematical calculations in their head. A famous example is Dustin Hoffman's character Raymond Babbitt in the film *Rain Man* (1988).

Asperger's Syndrome is slightly different from conventional autism, however, and has only recently been recognised as a distinctive condition. The main difference is that whereas autistic children have difficulties

---

[2] Peter Szatmari, 'Asperger's Disorder and Atypical Pervasive Developmental Disorder', in Fred R. Volkmar, ed., *Psychoses and Pervasive Developmental Disorders in Childhood and Adolescence*, American Psychiatric Press, Washington, D.C., 1996, pp.191-221.

[3] Mark Haddon, 'Mark Haddon Q&A', http://booktalk.guardian.co.uk/WebX?128@@.685ef53d

learning language, children with Asperger's Syndrome acquire language relatively easily, although they experience the same difficulties with social interactions.

The following list shows the 'diagnostic criteria' or signs that a child may have Asperger's Syndrome. You will notice that some, but not all, of these criteria fit Christopher Boone. Try to think of examples from the novel in each case.

- Difficulties in social interaction, including at least two of the following:
    - difficulties in using and understanding non-verbal forms of communication, such as eye-to-eye contact, facial expressions, body postures and gestures
    - difficulties in forming peer relationships
    - lack of a spontaneous desire to share enjoyment, interests or achievements with other people
    - lack of social or emotional reciprocity (two-way communication that involves showing an interest in others).
- Limited and repetitive patterns of behaviour, interests and activities, including at least one of the following:
    - highly intense or focused preoccupation with one or more narrow and repetitive interests
    - apparently inflexible adherence to specific, non-functional routines or rituals
    - characteristic repetitive gestures (for example, hand or finger flapping or twisting)
    - preoccupation with parts of objects.
    - Significant impairment in the development of social skills.
    - No significant delay in learning language.
    - No significant delay in intellectual development, self-help skills, adaptive abilities (apart from social interactions) or curiosity about the world.[4]

The incidence of Asperger's Syndrome is between 10 and 26 people per 100,000, roughly similar to the rates for conventional autism. Because research into Asperger's Syndrome is fairly recent, not much is known about long-term outcomes. Current research indicates that, after experiencing early difficulties with social interaction, children with Asperger's can gradually

---

[4] American Psychiatric Association, *Diagnostic and Statistical Manual of Mental Disorders: DSM-IV*, 4th edition, American Psychiatric Association, Washington, D.C., 1994, p.77.

improve with age. This seems to be the case with Christopher Boone, who notes in the chapter where he lists his Behavioural Problems that 'I don't have so many now because I'm more grown up' (p.59). However, it is likely that people with Asperger's will continue to have difficulties with social interaction throughout their lives.

Interestingly, Asperger's Syndrome appears to be almost entirely confined to boys, and one study shows that fathers of boys with Asperger's Syndrome often show behavioural problems similar to those of their sons. However, when Christopher's father says 'we're not that different, me and you' (pp.151-2), he seems to be referring specifically to the way in which they each have sudden outbursts of overpowering anger, rather than any broader issue.

A final point of interest is that one scientific explanation of autism proposes that autistic children 'lack a 'theory' of other people's minds. In other words, they cannot ascribe thoughts, feelings, or motivations to other people'.[5] This idea is explored in the scene when Julie, Christopher's teacher prior to Siobhan, tests Christopher by showing him a box of smarties which contains a pencil (p.145). When she asks Christopher what his mother would say if they asked her what was in the box, he replies 'A pencil'. As Christopher explains it, 'That was because when I was little I didn't understand about other people having minds'. However, he goes on to describe how he was able to overcome this problem:

> Julie said to Mother and Father that I would always find this very difficult. But I don't find this difficult now. Because I decided that it was a kind of puzzle, and if something is a puzzle there is always a way of solving it (p.145).

Christopher and Asperger's Syndrome

Although knowing a little bit about Asperger's Syndrome helps us to understand Christopher, we should not think that it 'explains' him entirely. He is much more than a collection of symptoms, and although he doesn't seem to have much sympathy for other people's feelings he clearly has an intense emotional life of his own, and we relate to him on this level. Once we get to know how his mind works, we can really identify with the anxiety and confusion he experiences on the journey to London and admire his courage in overcoming his fears.

---

[5] Szatmari, 'Asperger's Disorder and Atypical Pervasive Developmental Disorder', p.199.

As a narrator, Christopher doesn't label himself with medical terminology or see himself as having a disability. In other words, we should, and do, relate to Christopher as an interesting person who shows courage and intelligence in facing a series of challenging situations, rather than as someone who is so different from us as to be unknowable. Interestingly, Mark Haddon has said that some of Christopher's peculiarities are drawn from the peculiarities of 'normal' people that he knows:

> Christopher's character was, to a large extent, patched together by taking habits, opinions, patterns of thought and bits of behaviour from a range of people I know very well, none of whom would ever be labelled as having a disability (the maths, for example, is me; the refusal to eat different foods which are touching is my niece...and so on). But this reflects a deep truth, I think. No-one is ever really a stranger. We cling to the belief that we share nothing with certain people. It's rubbish. We have almost everything in common with everyone.[6]

Key point

Understanding Asperger's Syndrome from a medical perspective can deepen our insight into Christopher's experiences and, equally importantly, help us imagine more clearly the difficulties his parents must cope with. But ultimately it is Christopher's skill as storyteller, and the way he encourages us to see the world through his eyes, that brings these experiences to life in such a vivid and exciting way.

Sometimes it is possible to forget that Christopher is not a real person, but a fictional creation. But importantly, as Mark Haddon points out, 'if Christopher were real he couldn't / wouldn't have written the novel'.[7] Instead, the book is a work of imagination in which Mark Haddon has drawn on experience and insight to imagine himself 'inside the head' of someone with Asperger's Syndrome.

Therefore, it is interesting to read responses to *The Curious Incident...* by readers who have Asperger's Syndrome, or who have children with the condition. One parent writes that she could identify with Ed Boone and his problems in dealing with Christopher.[8] William Schofield, an 18-year-old with Asperger's, writes: 'I would say Christopher and I are pretty similar but I am older, more mature and more aware of the way the 'normal' world works'.[9] Another reviewer with Asperger's, Nicholas Barrow, found the book 'patronising, inaccurate and not entertaining', and complained that

---

[6] Haddon, 'Mark Haddon Q&A'.
[7] Haddon, 'Mark Haddon Q&A'.
[8] Haddon, 'Mark Haddon Q&A'.
[9] William Schofield, 'A Journey to shock and enlighten', *Guardian*, 29 January 2004.

people with Asperger's did not wet themselves and would definitely know what marzipan is.[10]

Mark Haddon sums up this range of responses:

> I have read criticism of the novel from a couple of people with Asperger's (you can find some on Amazon), mostly on the grounds that they don't recognise themselves, or other people they know with Asperger's, in Christopher. To which there are several answers...The first is that other people with Asperger's have found Christopher very convincing. The second is that Asperger's is a very broad definition and I don't think there's such a thing as a 'true' picture of someone with Asperger's, any more than there is a 'true' picture of a musician or a Norwegian. The third was put most succinctly by a good friend of mine who said, "It's not a novel about a boy with Asperger's, is it? It's a book about a young mathematician with some behavioural issues."[11]

GENRE, STRUCTURE & STYLE

Genre

Christopher says his book is 'a murder mystery novel' (p.5). He likes murder mysteries because detectives, like scientists, solve mysteries using precise observation and logical reasoning. The title of the novel comes from the story 'The Adventure of Silver Blaze', one of *The Adventures of Sherlock Holmes* by Sir Arthur Conan Doyle. What Sherlock Holmes refers to as 'the curious incident of the dog in the night-time'[12] is the fact that, during the theft of a racehorse in the middle of the night, the guard dog didn't bark, indicating that the thief was known to the dog. Sherlock Holmes uses this seemingly unimportant observation to solve the mystery.

Interestingly, classic detectives like Sherlock Holmes are often unemotional and antisocial, a little like people with Asperger's Syndrome. The novelist Jay McInerney makes this point in his review of the novel:

> One of the subtle ironies of the book, given the evolution of the murder mystery detective toward the tough guys of Hammett and Chandler, is that young Christopher is ultimately far more hard-boiled than any gumshoe in previous detective fiction: unlike Sam Spade or Nick Charles, he has no sentimental streak, no underground reservoir of emotional identification with other human beings.[13]

---

[10] 'Good questions, wicked answers,' *Guardian*, 7 June 2003

[11] Haddon, 'Mark Haddon Q&A'.

[12] Arthur Conan Doyle, *The Adventures of Sherlock Holmes*, Wordsworth Editions, Ware, 1995, p.303.

[13] Jay McInerney, 'The Remains of the Dog', *New York Times*, 15 June 2003, Section 7, p.5.

Only the first half of *The Curious Incident...* is a murder mystery, because in the middle of the book the murderer, Christopher's father, suddenly confesses (p.150). Although Christopher claims at the end of the novel to have solved the mystery, it is important to remember that he doesn't work it out for himself.

The second part of the novel is more like a quest narrative, in which the hero sets off on a journey in search of a goal and faces challenges that test their courage and ingenuity. At the end, the hero is transformed by their experience, having overcome their fears and discovered new skills and knowledge (a good example of a quest narrative is *The Lord of the Rings*).

A third important genre is the *Bildungsroman*. Based on the German words *Bildung = growth and development* and *roman = novel*, the *Bildungsroman* focuses on one character and tells the story of that person's childhood, education, growth and development into maturity. One of the profound questions the novel raises is whether Christopher really matures in the course of the narrative. He certainly learns to cope with a number of situations he had previously found frightening or impossible, and at the end of the novel he comes out of his shell to help his mother and father with household chores. But at the same time, he still seems to be emotionally disconnected, more preoccupied with mathematics than with the lives of the people around him.

A Two-Part Structure

The Curious Incident... is in two parts. The first part deals with Christopher's investigation and the second part with the discovery that his mother is alive and his journey to London. In the middle section of the novel (Chapters 149 to 167) these two storylines overlap.

One of the first things the reader notices is that the novel begins with Chapter 2. Christopher numbers his chapters with prime numbers (2, 3, 5, 7, 11, 13) because he likes prime numbers: 'I think prime numbers are like life. They are very logical but you could never work out the rules, even if you spent all your time thinking about them' (p.15).

The chapters follow a regular pattern, alternating between episodes that move the story along and 'inter-chapters' that contain entertaining digressions. These digressions explore a range of seemingly irrelevant topics that are important to Christopher. Mark Haddon notes that:

> As a narrator Christopher likes to say precisely what happened and have done with it. The digressions helped slow up this headlong rush and give the reader another insight into the workings of his mind.[14]

Sometimes these inter-chapters consist of flashbacks on important events in Christopher's past, such as Chapters 43 and 53 which deal with the supposed death of his mother.

Style

Literal and Metaphoric Language

Christopher's use of language is very literal, reflected in the usually short, factual nature of his sentences. He doesn't tell lies because it makes his head hurt to think about things that didn't happen (p.24), and he doesn't like novels 'because they are lies about things which didn't happen and they make me feel shaky and scared' (p.25).

Christopher also doesn't like things that have different layers of meaning, like jokes (p.10) or facial expressions (p.19). For this reason, Christopher doesn't like metaphors. A metaphor is 'when you describe something by using a word for something that it isn't' (p.20). For Christopher, a metaphor is a lie. Discussing the metaphor 'he was the apple of her eye', Christopher says:

> when I try and make a picture of the phrase in my head it just confuses me because imagining an apple in someone's eye doesn't have anything to do with liking someone a lot and it makes you forget what the person was talking about (p.20).

Rather than metaphors, Christopher prefers similes, comparisons between two things that are literally similar, like the policeman's hairy nose that 'looked as if there were two very small mice hiding in his nostrils' (p.22). Throughout the book, Christopher carefully points out whenever he is using a simile.

Structural Irony

Irony refers to a statement that has two levels of meaning: a surface level of literal meaning, and a hidden *ironic* meaning implied by the speaker, often the opposite of the literal meaning. Because of his dislike of ambiguity, Christopher Boone is unable to understand irony: he takes every statement on face value and always says exactly what he means.

---

[14] Haddon, 'Mark Haddon Q&A'

However, the novel itself is ironic because it contains layers of meaning that Christopher is unaware of. For example, Christopher says 'This will not be a funny book' (p.10), but it *is* a funny book, precisely because Christopher describes things in such a deadpan way.

This technique involves what is called structural irony. The following definition seems to fit *The Curious Incident*... rather well:

> Some literary works exhibit structural irony, in that they show sustained irony...One common device of this sort is the invention of a naïve hero, or else a naïve narrator or spokesman, whose invincible simplicity or obtuseness leads him to persist in putting an interpretation on affairs which the knowing reader...is called on to alter and correct.[15]

Structural irony can be both comic and tragic in its effects. We might find Christopher's attempts to 'do chatting' with Mrs Alexander amusing (p.51), although Christopher of course would be very offended if he thought we were laughing at him. But there is sometimes a tragic edge to this irony, such as when Christopher's father lies to him about his mother dying and Christopher says 'it was nice, having Father speak to me but not look at me' (p.29).

The Unreliable Narrator

Christopher's inability to understand emotions means that he is an 'unreliable narrator'. Unreliable narrators are first-person narrators whose narratives present a partial and sometimes misleading version of events. This may be because they are biased against some characters, or because they wish to exaggerate their own importance, or because, like Christopher, they lack insight into the motives and actions of others. Modern novelists often use unreliable narrators to remind us that our knowledge of other people is always limited by our point of view, in terms of both what we know about them and how we feel about them.[16]

In *The Curious Incident...*, Christopher rarely describes people's faces but often focuses on their clothes, and especially on aspects of their shoes, such as the orange leaf stuck to the policeman's shoe (p.7) or Mrs Alexander's 'New Balance trainers' (p.50). These details remind us

---

[15] M.H. Abrams, *A Glossary of Literary Terms*, CBS Publishing, New York, 1981, p.90.

[16] A famous example of an unreliable narrator is Nick Carraway, the narrator of F. Scott Fitzgerald's *The Great Gatsby* (1925). From various clues the reader notices that, through his admiration for Gatsby, Carraway tends to skim over the 'dark side' of Gatsby's character, giving a biased portrait of Gatsby as a tragic hero.

that Christopher does not like looking at people's faces. Because of this, Christopher's narrative lacks the interpretive commentary on other people's emotions that we usually expect from a narrator; we share Christopher's limited perspective.

However, this does not mean Christopher is a bad narrator – he is highly observant and has an excellent memory. Even though he doesn't understand gestures, he observes and records them. For instance, Christopher says he doesn't know what it means when people breathe out loudly through their nose (p.19), but when he describes the policeman doing this at the police station a few pages later (p.23) the reader knows that the policeman is expressing weary exasperation, even if Christopher doesn't.

A final important aspect of Christopher as a narrator is that, because he doesn't have an emotional 'involvement' with other people, he doesn't seem to pass judgment or take sides: he tells us only what he sees and hears.

CHAPTER-BY-CHAPTER ANALYSIS

Chapter 2 (p.1)

Straight away we notice something unusual about this novel because it starts at Chapter 2. This is not immediately explained. The novel begins with Christopher's discovery of a dead dog pierced by a garden fork. Christopher gives the exact time – 'It was 7 minutes after midnight' (p.1) – and the tone of his description is detached, precise and logical. Christopher reasons that the dog was probably killed with the fork because it is unlikely that anyone would stick a fork into a dead dog, although he 'could not be certain about this' (p.1).

Chapter 3 (Inter-chapter) (pp.2-3)

This chapter does not continue the narrative of the first chapter, and marks the start of a pattern that continues through the novel. Christopher alternates between chapters that advance the story, and 'inter-chapters' that tell the reader about Christopher and the things that interest him.

Christopher boastfully announces to the reader: 'My name is Christopher John Francis Boone. I know all the countries of the world and their capital cities and every prime number up to 7,507' (p.2). He goes on to describe how he understands the happy and sad faces that Siobhan shows him, but doesn't understand the other facial expressions. (Many readers may also find the other facial expressions confusing.) We begin to sense that Christopher is someone who is highly intelligent in terms of logic, memory and mathematics, but not so strong in the 'emotional intelligence' that many people take for granted. Importantly, he shows that he is aware of this.

Many readers will find amusing the idea of Christopher trying to use diagrams to understand people's faces. Siobhan finds this funny, but Christopher gets upset with her and she apologises. This brief scene introduces the ironic comedy that arises from Christopher's deadpan descriptions of his unusual experiences. But it also warns the reader that Christopher does not like being laughed at and wishes to be respected despite his differences.

Chapter 5 (p.4)

Christopher explains that he likes dogs because they only have four moods, 'Happy, sad, cross and concentrating' (p.4), and because they are faithful and do not tell lies. This introduces an important theme in the novel: Christopher knows that people are sometimes unfaithful and tell lies, but he has no way of protecting himself against this because he can't 'read' other people's faces or moods.

Christopher describes how Mrs Shears comes outside to find him hugging the dead dog, and screams at him "What in fuck's name have you done to my dog?" (p.4). Christopher reports everything he hears exactly, without 'editing out' the bad language. He puts down the dog, and when Mrs Shears starts screaming he puts his hands over his ears, closes his eyes and rolls forward until his forehead touches the grass. He describes this as if it is a perfectly normal reaction. Thus the reader begins to learn what it is like to be Christopher Boone.

Chapter 7 (Inter-chapter) (pp.5-6)

Christopher announces: 'This is a murder mystery novel' (p.7). He goes on to describe Siobhan and Mr Jeavons (but not his father) and explains how Siobhan is helping him write his book. He also explains that he finds it hard to imagine things that didn't happen, which is why he is telling the story of finding the dead dog – because it really happened to him, even though it is usually people who are killed in murder mysteries. Christopher repeats that he cares about dogs because they are faithful and honest, and says that some dogs are cleverer and more interesting than some people, such as Steve at his school. We begin to see the streak of arrogance and insensitivity that is a part of Christopher's character.

Chapter 11 (pp.7-9)

The police arrive and ask Christopher about what happened. He says he likes policemen because 'they have uniforms and numbers and you know what they are meant to be doing' (p.7). However, Christopher becomes confused by the questions: 'They were stacking up in my head like loaves in the factory where Uncle Terry works' (p.8). Again Christopher copes with his confusion by rolling forward and pressing his forehead on the grass:

> I…made the noise that Father calls groaning. I make this noise when there is too much information coming into my head from the outside world (p.8).

The policeman doesn't understand what Christopher is doing or why, and tries to lift him to his feet, but Christopher does not like to be touched and so hits the policeman.

Chapter 13 (Inter-chapter) (p.10)

Christopher explains 'This will not be a funny book' since 'I cannot tell jokes because I do not understand them' (p.10). However, readers notice the irony here, because the book is funny, but the humour arises from Christopher's deadpan narration.

Christopher explains that he cannot understand jokes (by which he means puns) because he finds it 'uncomfortable and confusing' when a word means two or three different things at the same time (p.10). Christopher does not like ambiguity; he likes things to be ordered and definite.

Chapter 17 (pp.11-13)

The policeman arrests Christopher for assaulting a police officer. Christopher says 'This made me feel a lot calmer because it is what policemen say on television and in films' (p.11). Rather than worrying about being arrested, Christopher is relieved that the policeman is doing what policemen do.

While he is in the police car Christopher looks at the sky. The second half of this chapter is a discussion of the Big Bang theory of the universe. Christopher loves scientific explanations, and his discussion of the eventual extinction of life on earth is scientifically dispassionate.

Chapter 19 (Inter-chapter) (pp.14-15)

Christopher finally explains that he has numbered his chapters exclusively with prime numbers simply 'because I like prime numbers' (p.14). He explains a process for working out prime numbers by eliminating composite numbers (called Eratosthenes' Sieve). He thinks prime numbers are like life: 'They are very logical but you could never work out the rules' (p.15).

Chapter 23 (pp.16-18)

Christopher is taken to the police station, where he is asked to empty his pockets. He gives a precise list of their contents, including his beloved Swiss Army Knife. Christopher explains to the police that he needs to keep his watch on because he needs to know exactly what time it is, and when they try to take it off him he screams. This is another instance of Christopher's odd behaviour, but because it is described in a matter-of-fact way, and because Christopher quickly moves on to the next incident, we start to accept this behaviour as understandable; we start to identify with Christopher as a character.

The police ask Christopher about his family, and this is where we learn his mother is dead (p.17). He gives the police his father's phone numbers and is taken to a cell, where he is quite happy because it is almost a perfect cube, and because everything in it has a purpose.

Chapter 29 (Inter-chapter) (pp.19-20)

This is an important chapter, because it tells us a lot about Christopher. He says: 'I find people confusing' (p.19) and gives two reasons.

The first reason is that 'people do a lot of talking without using any words' (p.19). One of the characteristic features of Asperger's Syndrome is difficulty in interpreting non-verbal forms of communication such as facial expressions and gestures. Whereas most people develop an instinctive 'sense' for body language, Christopher tries to work out the meanings of non-verbal signals through logic, which is impossible. Gestures such as raising an eyebrow or breathing out through your nose are confusing because they can mean many different things.

The second reason Christopher finds people confusing is that they often talk using metaphors. Christopher defines metaphor as 'when you describe something by using a word for something that it isn't' (p.20). This is another example of Christopher's preference for literal and unambiguous communication. Christopher is not happy that his own name is a metaphor that refers to the biblical character who carried Jesus Christ across a river. He insists that: 'I do not want my name to mean a story about being kind and helpful. I want my name to mean me' (p.20).

Christopher wants language to be literal and unambiguous. But language is much more complicated, and puns, ambiguities, metaphors and irony are part of the richness of language that many people take pleasure in, even though Christopher finds them disturbing.

Chapter 31 (pp.21-3)

Christopher's father comes to the police station to collect him. When Christopher is released we see that his dislike of being touched extends even to hugging his father. They make the gesture of touching their outspread fingers together, which 'means that he loves me' (p.21).

The policeman interviews Christopher and gives him a caution. Christopher tells the policeman "I always tell the truth" (p.23), and we see proof of this when the policeman wants to record a 'white lie' that the assault was an accident. Christopher insists that "it wasn't an accident", which causes the policeman to exhale through his nose (p.23).

Key point

The policeman's gesture is confusing to Christopher, but most readers will easily interpret it as a sign of exasperation. This is an example of the way Christopher, through precise observation and his excellent memory, is able to give the reader clues to layers of meaning that he himself does not understand.

Chapter 37 (Inter-chapter) (pp.24-5)

This is another important inter-chapter because here Christopher explains how he feels about lies:

> I do not tell lies. Mother used to say that this was because I was a good person. But it is not because I am a good person. It is because I can't tell lies (p.24).

For Christopher, telling lies is not a moral issue but a conceptual one. His mind seems incapable of dealing with statements that are untrue. He imagines telling a lie about what he had for breakfast, and shows how the rapid build-up of imaginary possibilities makes him feel 'shaky and scared' (p.24). Christopher insists: 'everything I have written here is true' (p.25).

Chapter 41 (pp.26-7)

On the way home from the police station Christopher tells his father that he is going to find out who killed Wellington. His father tells him repeatedly to "keep your nose out of other people's business" (p.26), eventually banging the steering wheel of the car in frustration and shouting, "I said leave it, for God's sake" (p.27).

Christopher's lack of emotional insight means that he doesn't realise his father is angry until he loses his temper: 'I could tell he was angry because he was shouting' (p.27). It also means that he doesn't see anything unusual in his father's sensitivity to this issue, whereas a more intuitive detective might have seen something suspicious here. Later, when he sees his father crying, Christopher innocently asks whether he is sad about Wellington. His father answers, "You could say that" (p.27). Christopher decides to go upstairs to his room 'because when I am sad I want to be alone' (p.27).

Key point

These two scenes show that Christopher can be sensitive to other people's emotions, but only at a relatively simple level (angry, sad), and only when the signs of those emotions are clear (shouting, crying). Christopher does not suspect that there are bigger and more complex issues behind his father's tears than simple grief over the death of Wellington.

Chapter 43 (Inter-chapter) (pp.28-30)

This the first of three inter-chapters in which Christopher tells the story of his mother's death.

One day, two years earlier, Christopher came home to an empty house. Later, his father asked him if he had seen his mother, made a series of phone calls and went out for a while. When he returned he told Christopher a lie: that his mother had gone to hospital. Christopher's father avoided looking at him when he told this lie, but Christopher suspected nothing because, ironically, Christopher doesn't like people looking at him when they talk to him. In fact, Christopher thought it was 'nice, having Father speak to me but not look at me' (p.29).

When Christopher was told that his mother was in hospital he wasn't upset, but on the contrary was excited about going to the hospital to visit her because 'I like the uniforms and the machines' (p.29).

Chapter 47 (pp.31-4)

Christopher explains that the next day is a 'Good Day', a day for projects, which is the day that he begins writing his story. He explains the system of Quite Good Days, Good Days and Super Good Days, which depend on whether he sees three, four or five red cars in a row. Four yellow cars in a row make it a 'Black Day', when Christopher doesn't speak to anyone or eat anything and 'Take[s] No Risks' (p.31).

Christopher describes a conversation with Mr Jeavons, the psychologist at his school, in which Mr Jeavons is surprised by Christopher's seemingly illogical system. Christopher explains that he likes things to be in a nice order, and his system provides this.

Christopher also discusses his ambition of becoming an astronaut, but admits that it is unlikely to happen. But he insists 'I'm not a spazzer' (p.33) and that he will go to university to study Mathematics or Physics.

Chapter 53 (Inter-chapter) (pp.35-7)

This is the second inter-chapter concerning Christopher's mother's death. Two weeks after his mother supposedly went to hospital, his father told him that she died of a heart attack. Christopher, in his scientific way, wished to know whether it was an aneurysm or an embolism, but his father was unable to answer this question. Christopher accepted this and didn't notice anything strange or suspicious. That evening Mrs Shears cooked supper for them, and Christopher describes how she stood next to Christopher's father, held his head against her breasts and said "Come on, Ed. We're going to get you through this" (p.37). Readers might suspect that Christopher's father and Mrs Shears were starting to have an affair, but Christopher did not notice.

Chapter 59 (pp.38-41)

Christopher decides to go ahead with his investigation, even though his father has told him not to. He says he doesn't always do what he is told because the orders people give him don't always make sense. He says he likes the way Siobhan gives him instructions because she is always very specific, but other people don't understand this. However, Christopher seems to know that what he is doing is wrong, and to be deliberately disobeying his father's instructions.

Christopher goes to see Mrs Shears, who refuses to talk to him. Then he decides to 'do some detective work' (p.40) by examining Mrs Shears's toolshed. When Mrs Shears finds him she threatens to call the police, so he goes home.

Chapter 61 (Inter-chapter) (pp.42-4)

Christopher explains that he doesn't believe in heaven because it isn't logical. Reverend Peters is unable to give a description of God or heaven that fits Christopher's scientific knowledge of the universe. Although he didn't go to his mother's funeral, Christopher knows she was cremated and he likes to imagine that her ashes have become part of the air. This shows that, in his own scientific way, Christopher misses his mother.

Chapter 67 (pp.45-55)

While his father is watching soccer on television, Christopher decides to do some more detective work by interviewing people in his street. He explains that he ordinarily doesn't like talking to strangers and that his fear of people touching him can make him react violently. However, he reasons that 'if you are going to do detective work you have to be brave, so I had no choice' (p.46).

Christopher proceeds systematically down the street, at first with little success. But eventually he strikes up a conversation with Mrs Alexander, an elderly woman who lives opposite. She manages to engage him in conversation even though he doesn't like 'chatting', and he even tries to 'do chatting' himself by saying "My age is 15 years and 3 months and 3 days" (p.51). She offers him cake and orange squash, but while she is inside he starts thinking she might phone the police and walks away.

Christopher develops a 'Chain of Reasoning' and decides that Mr Shears is his 'Prime Suspect' (pp.53-4). However, in the course of his reasoning Christopher tells the reader that, after Mr Shears left Mrs Shears two years ago, Mrs Shears used to come over and spend the night with Christopher's father. Christopher is unable to 'put two and two together', but the reader now has no doubt that Christopher's father and Mrs Shears were having an affair.

Chapter 71 (Inter-chapter) (pp.56-8)

Christopher complains that the other children at his school are stupid. He also makes fun of the politically correct term 'Special Needs' (p.56), arguing that everybody has special needs of one kind or another, and in any case the children from the school down the road simply turn 'Special Needs!' into a term of abuse.

Christopher tells of his ambition to sit his A level Maths exam, and describes how his father stood up for Christopher's right to sit this exam.

Chapter 73 (Inter-chapter) (pp.59-61)

Christopher tells how his mother and father often fought 'because of the stress of looking after someone who has Behavioural Problems like I have' (p.59). But he also says he has fewer problems than he used to. He lists his Behavioural Problems, some of which the reader is already familiar with. He tells us how his behaviour would make his parents angry, and we begin to feel sympathy for what his parents have had to cope with. Christopher doesn't excuse himself for his behaviour, which he sees as beyond his control. He takes it as a fact of life and part of who he is.

Chapter 79 (pp.62-4)

Christopher comes home and tells his father a white lie about where he has been. Although Christopher tries to justify this to himself, it is clear that he knows he is deliberately deceiving his father. Christopher's father has received a phone call from Mrs Shears, and knows what Christopher has been up to. Once again, Christopher takes a long time to realise that his father is angry. His father says that Mr Shears "is evil" and that Mrs Shears is "not a friend any more" (p.63), indicating (to the reader, if not to Christopher) that their affair has ended. Christopher wants to continue asking questions, but his father makes him promise to "stop this ridiculous bloody detective game" (p.64).

Chapter 83 (Inter-chapter) (pp.65-6)

Christopher explains that he would make a very good astronaut because he is intelligent, understands machines and likes being alone.

Chapter 89 (pp.67-8)

Christopher explains to Siobhan that his book is finished because he is not allowed to do any more detecting. He is disappointed, because he would like his book to end with the solving of the mystery. He also tells Siobhan what his father said about Mr and Mrs Shears, but Siobhan does not know his family and is unable to help him.

Chapter 97 (pp.69-77)

Christopher sees five red cars in a row, making it a 'Super Good Day' (p.69). He sees Mrs Alexander again and does his best to 'do chatting' by saying things like "I like maths and looking after Toby. And also I like outer space and I like being on my own" (p.71). Feeling that she might be able to help him with his investigation, Christopher asks her why his father called Mr Shears an evil man. Once again, Christopher does some dishonest reasoning to justify why this does not count as breaking his promise, showing that he is starting to learn that the distinction between truth and lies is not always clear-cut.

Mrs Alexander advises Christopher to stop asking questions about Mr Shears, saying, "I think you know why your father doesn't like Mr Shears very much" (p.73). Christopher has no idea what she means, so Mrs Alexander spells it out to him until he understands that his mother and Mr Shears were "doing sex" (p.76).

Chapter 101 (Inter-chapter) (pp.78-82)

Christopher reports a conversation with the school psychologist, Mr Jeavons. Mr Jeavons suggests that Christopher likes maths because it is safe, because the problems always have a straightforward answer: 'What he meant was that maths wasn't like life because in life there are no straightforward answers at the end' (p.76). Christopher gives an explanation of the Monty Hall Problem to show that maths isn't always as straightforward as Mr Jeavons thinks.

The fact that even professional mathematicians got the relatively simple Monty Hall Problem wrong shows, for Christopher, that 'intuition can sometimes get things wrong…But logic can help you to work out the right answer' (p.82).

Key point

The placement of this chapter is ironic, because Christopher's lack of intuition meant that he had no idea about his mother's affair with Mr Shears or his father's affair with Mrs Shears. Logic alone without intuition can also lead to wrong answers.

Chapter 103 (pp.83-7)

Christopher describes an evening at home with his father and his father's employee Rhodri. He gives a detailed description of the night sky viewed from the garden, and explains how Siobhan has helped him with his story by suggesting he describe people using one or two details 'so that people could make a picture of them in their head' (p.85).

Chapter 107 (Inter-chapter) (pp.88-93)

Christopher summarises his favourite book, *The Hound of the Baskervilles*.

Christopher admires Sherlock Holmes because he is very intelligent and solves mysteries, and says things like 'The world is full of obvious things which nobody by any chance observes' (p.92). Christopher feels that he is like Sherlock Holmes, both in being observant and in having 'the power of detaching his mind at will' (p.92). However, Christopher's assessments of his powers of observation continue to be ironic, since he overlooks so many things that are 'obvious' to the reader.

Chapter 109 (pp.94-5)

The next day Christopher continues work on his book at school. Siobhan, reading the book, asks if Christopher is upset by the news that his mother was having an affair. Christopher, in his logical and unemotional way, answers that he isn't upset because that "would be feeling sad about something that isn't real and doesn't exist. And that would be stupid" (p.95).

Chapter 113 (Inter-chapter) (pp.96-9)

Christopher says 'My memory is like a film' (p.96), and describes how he can rewind to different scenes and replay them in detail. He gives an example of a memory of being at the beach with his mother. He also explains how he does a 'Search' to work out what to do, such as taking appropriate action if someone at school is having an epileptic fit (pp.97-8).

Christopher makes the point that his head only contains memories of things that actually happened, whereas 'other people have pictures in their heads of things which aren't real and didn't happen' (p.98). Christopher can't understand why people have worries or regrets; his mind is very concrete, focused on facts.

Chapter 127 (pp.100-4)

Christopher is watching one of his favourite videos when his father comes in and discovers the book detailing Christopher's investigation. He asks Christopher, "What is this?" but 'he said it very quietly and I didn't realise that he was angry because he wasn't shouting' (p.101). Christopher's father asks why he has continued his investigation, and Christopher responds with his ingenious explanation of why he hasn't disobeyed his father's instructions. However, Christopher's father doesn't accept this argument: "You knew exactly what you were bloody doing" (p.102).

Christopher's father loses his temper and grabs Christopher by the arm. As earlier with the policeman, Christopher responds by lashing out, but then there is a period in which Christopher 'blacks out': 'It was like someone had switched me off and then switched me on again' (p.103). Christopher comes to with an aching head and blood on his hand, while his father is scratched and his shirt is torn. Christopher watches his father go out the back door and drop something into the rubbish bin.

Chapter 131 (Inter-chapter) (pp.105-7)

Christopher explains why he hates yellow and brown. He admits that hating yellow and brown 'is sort of being silly' (p.105), but Christopher has trouble making decisions in everyday life so hating some things makes the decisions easier.

Chapter 137 (pp.108-10)

To say he is sorry, Christopher's father takes Christopher on an expedition to Twycross Zoo. While they are eating lunch his father apologises for 'losing his rag' (p.109), and tells Christopher that he loves him. He asks Christopher whether he understands and Christopher says yes, because his father 'always tells me the truth, which means that he loves me' (p.109). This speech takes on a sad irony because Christopher soon learns that his father has lied to him about his mother's death. The chapter ends with Christopher showing off his photographic memory by drawing a map of the zoo.

Chapter 139 (Inter-chapter) (pp.111-13)

Christopher dislikes people who believe in the supernatural. He is critical even of his favourite author, Sir Arthur Conan Doyle, because Doyle believed you could communicate with the dead. Christopher illustrates his point with the famous trick photograph of the Cottingley Fairies, and says that people like Doyle who were taken in by the hoax were 'being stupid' (p.112). For Christopher, cases like this show that 'sometimes people want to be stupid and they do not want to know the truth' (p.113).

Chapter 149 (pp.114-24)

At school on Monday Siobhan notices the bruise on Christopher's face and asks him about the fight with his father, but importantly she respects Christopher's independence and doesn't press him any further.

When he gets home Christopher decides to 'do some detecting' (p.115) to try to find his book. He eventually finds it in a box in a cupboard in his father's room. When he hears his father's van pull up, he quickly decides to leave the book where it is, but then he notices a pile of envelopes all addressed to Christopher Boone. He takes one and hides it under his mattress before going downstairs.

Later that evening Christopher reads the first of the letters from his mother. It is written from London, where she has just got a new job as a secretary in a factory. She writes about recently moving house with a man called Roger to a new flat in Willesden. She ends the letter by writing: 'You haven't written to me yet, so I know that you are probably still angry with me. I'm sorry Christopher. But I still love you' (p.122). Christopher checks the postmark of the letter, and sees that it was posted eighteen months after his mother was supposed to have died.

Christopher's father comes in and asks him what he is doing; Christopher answers simply "I'm reading a letter" (p.123). This is another 'white lie', but we might have expected Christopher to tell an outright lie here. Christopher's father doesn't seem to think it unusual that Christopher is reading a letter, but this scene shows in a subtle way that Christopher finds it difficult to tell lies.

Christopher is very confused by his discovery. He still believes that his mother is dead, so he is unable to explain this mystery: 'I was excited. When I started writing my book there was only one mystery I had to solve. Now there were two' (p.124). He hides the letter again and decides to wait for an opportunity to read the other letters.

Chapter 151 (Inter-chapter) (pp.125-8)

For Christopher, all mysteries have an explanation and science will eventually find explanations for unexplained phenomena such as ghosts. He gives an example of a mystery that really isn't a mystery, the fluctuations in the population of frogs in the school pond. He gives a mathematical equation for predicting animal populations, taken from James Gleick's *Chaos* which he mentions reading in the previous chapter (p.120). Christopher explains how the graph of the equation can fluctuate wildly, reflecting the fact that a whole population can die out suddenly for no reason 'just because that is the way the numbers work' (p.128).

Chapter 157 (pp.129-44)

It is not until the following Monday that Christopher gets a chance to read the other letters. There are 43 letters, all addressed to him in the same handwriting.

In the first letter, Christopher's mother mentions a happy memory of when she and Christopher's father gave him a train set. She reminisces about how Christopher was fascinated with train timetables, and always made the trains run on time. Christopher later draws on this memory for help during the trip to London.

In the second, longer letter, Christopher's mother writes to explain why she went away. She says 'I was not a very good mother' because she has a short temper, whereas 'Your father is a much more pacient person' (p.133). She describes an incident during a shopping trip when Christopher had a panic attack, knocked some mixers off a shelf and then lay on the ground screaming. She had waited until he stopped screaming and they then had to walk home because Christopher refused to get on the bus. That evening she was very upset and told Christopher's father she couldn't cope any more, which led to an argument in which she hit him.

She then tells how she and Christopher's father stopped talking to each other and she started to feel lonely. She started having a relationship with Roger Shears, but when he suggested they move in together she said no because of Christopher. However, she and Christopher had a fight because he had not eaten for days and she was trying to make him eat. He threw a chopping board at her that broke her toes, and while she was recovering Christopher's father looked after him. She started to feel left out, 'like you didn't really need me at all' (p.136). At this time Roger was transferred to London and Christopher's mother impulsively decided to go with him. She says that she meant to see Christopher in order to say goodbye and explain what she was doing, but that Christopher's father wouldn't let her. She says 'I thought that what I was doing was the best for all of us' (p.137), and she pleads with Christopher to write back to her or ring her. Clearly, though, she has not properly thought through the implications of her actions.

In the third letter, Mrs Boone writes about the office where she works, and mentions a present she has sent Christopher, a mathematical puzzle.

In the course of reading the fourth letter Christopher starts to feel sick. He realises that 'Mother had been alive all the time. And Father had lied about this' (p.141). He can't think clearly because his 'brain wasn't working properly' (p.141), so he curls up in a ball. There is a gap in his memory where a long time passes, because when he opens his eyes again it is dark and he is covered in vomit. He hears his father come into the room and say "Christopher, what the hell are you doing", but his voice 'sounded tiny and far away' (p.142). Christopher's father realises that Christopher has discovered the letters, and apologises, echoing the words of Christopher's mother's letters when he says: "I did it for your good, Christopher. Honestly I did. I never meant to lie. I just thought…that it was better if you didn't know" (p.143).

Christopher's father helps Christopher get cleaned up, undressing him and leading him to the bathroom, and for once, because he is in a state of shock, Christopher doesn't mind being touched: 'I didn't scream. And I didn't fight. And I didn't hit him' (p.144). This chapter shows Christopher's devastation in finding out that his father has lied to him, as well as demonstrating his father's patience and gentleness in trying to help Christopher cope with this news.

Chapter 163 (Inter-chapter) (pp.145-8)

Christopher tells a story about a test he did with his former teacher Julie, which showed that when he was younger he 'didn't understand about other people having minds' (p.145). Even though Julie told Christopher's parents he would always find it difficult to understand other people, Christopher decided he could overcome this problem by making it into a puzzle for himself, because 'if something is a puzzle there is always a way of solving it' (p.145).

Christopher then explains why people's brains are like computers. He says people think their brains are special because computers don't have feelings. But Christopher tries to explain feelings as a kind of cognitive skill or thought process:

> feelings are just having a picture on the screen in your head of what is going to happen tomorrow or next year, or what might have happened instead of what did happen, and if it is a happy picture they smile and if it is a sad picture they cry (p.148).

Chapter 167 (pp.149-55)

Christopher remains in a trance-like state, not responding to his father but doubling 2s in his head to calm himself down. His father tells him that from now on he will always tell the truth, and then goes on to confess that he killed Wellington (p.150). At first Christopher thinks it is a joke, but his father goes on to explain how it happened and by the end Christopher says 'And then I knew that it wasn't a joke and I was really frightened' (p.152). When his father tries to touch him he screams, pushing his father away. Christopher thinks that his father might try to murder him and decides he must get away. He waits until his father falls asleep, then takes Toby and his special food box, sneaks out of the house and hides behind the garden shed.

In Christopher's father's 'confession' (pp.151-2) he tries to explain to Christopher how he felt about Mrs Shears. He thought she might eventually move in with him and Christopher but then they started having arguments, and after a particularly nasty argument she threw him out of the house. He describes the moment of rage that led him to kill the dog, comparing it to one of Christopher's outbursts:

> "when that red mist comes down…Christ, you know how it is. I mean, we're not that different, me and you…it was like everything I'd been bottling up for two years just…" (pp.151-2).

Christopher's father is having an emotional crisis. His wife left him two years earlier, and he has had to cope single-handedly with bringing up a son who is unable to return his affection and who has difficult behavioural problems. When his relationship with Mrs Shears broke down, Ed Boone had been overwhelmed by pent-up emotions of disappointment, frustration and loneliness, and in a fit of rage killed Mrs Shears's dog.

Key point

This action is the catalyst for the first half of the novel, and the novel as a whole can be seen as shaped by the working-through of Christopher's father's emotional crisis. In fact, we could describe the novel as the story of a loving father's emotional breakdown and his attempts to gain redemption, but described in a curiously unemotional way from the perspective of his autistic son.

Chapter 173 (Inter-chapter) (pp.156-7)

Christopher talks about the constellation Orion and the highly arbitrary way people group clusters of stars into constellations. To contrast with the previous chapter, he finishes with the words 'And that is the truth' (p.157).

Chapter 179 (pp.158-73)

Christopher spends the night hiding behind the garden shed. In the morning he hears his father come out looking for him and then drive away in his van. He decides to go and live with Mrs Shears, a decision that shows his complete lack of understanding of the situation. Luckily Mrs Shears isn't in, so Christopher hides around the side of her house and tries to decide what to do.

Christopher's decision-making process shows how difficult it can be to make important decisions based only on logic rather than intuition and emotional insight. He realises that 'there was nothing I could do which felt safe' (p.162), but by eliminating other options he decides he will catch the train to London to live with his mother. Once he has *'Formulated a Plan'* (p.164) he feels better.

He asks Mrs Alexander to look after Toby, but when she suggests they ring his father he runs away and is almost knocked over by a car. He breaks into his house, finds his father's wallet on the kitchen bench and takes his father's bank card.

The next step in his plan is to go to school and ask Siobhan to help him catch the train to London, another decision that shows he doesn't understand how adults will react to his plan to go to London on his own. When he sees his father's van at the school he is so afraid that he vomits. He uses Siobhan's technique of counting fifty deep breaths to calm down (p.169), showing that he is already learning to cope with stressful situations on his own. Eventually, after a series of challenges, he manages to find the train station.

Chapter 181 (Inter-chapter) (pp.174-8)

Christopher says 'I see everything' (p.174) and goes on to describe his extraordinary powers of perception. Using the example of standing in a field in the countryside, he shows how he takes in and remembers every detail of his surroundings. He doesn't like new places because they present an overload of new information, 'like when a computer is doing too many things at the same time and the central processor unit is blocked up and there isn't any space left to think about other things' (p.177). In other words, Christopher doesn't possess the ability to 'edit out' new information to focus on what is most important or relevant. As a result, he gets confused by crowds and unfamiliar places, and copes by putting his hands over his eyes and groaning.

Chapter 191 (pp.179-91)

Christopher gives a detailed map of the train station, apologising that it is only an 'approximation' because he was too scared to notice things properly (p.179). He sits down at a table to gather his thoughts and does a maths problem called Conway's Soldiers to calm himself down.

He is questioned by a policeman in the first of a series of encounters with the police. Christopher explains who he is and where he is going, but tells white lies about how he will get money for a ticket. As they go to the cashpoint machine together, Christopher tells the policeman not to touch him, another sign that he is learning ways to cope with his behavioural problems. The policeman helps him use the cash machine and directs him to the ticket office, where he eventually succeeds in buying a ticket and getting on the train to London.

In these scenes Christopher learns different ways to cope with new situations. He imagines he is playing a computer game; he also imagines a red line across the floor that leads where he wants to go, and he says 'Left, right' to himself in a rhythmic way, another trick Siobhan has taught him (p.190). Other coping mechanisms, like barking at people to scare them off (p.190), are not so positive.

Chapter 193 (Inter-chapter) (pp.192-5)

We have already seen that Christopher always likes to know the exact time. In this chapter he explains why he likes timetables, and that he hates holidays because people don't have a timetable on holidays. He discusses the theory of relativity and describes how timetables 'make sure you don't get lost in time' (p.195).

Chapter 197 (pp.196-202)

Christopher starts the chapter describing how he hates being in confined spaces with other people, which explains why he dislikes being on the train. The policeman follows Christopher onto the train and tries to take him back to his father at the police station, but the train pulls out with both of them still aboard. Christopher takes the opportunity of going to the toilet to hide in a luggage rack, where he solves quadratic equations in his head to calm down. The policeman looks for Christopher but does not find him.

Chapter 199 (Inter-chapter) (pp.203-4)

Christopher again discusses the existence of God, suggesting that people believe in God because it seems too unlikely that human beings could have evolved simply by accident. To argue against this belief, Christopher discusses the theory of evolution and shows how genetics can explain the evolution of human beings.

Chapter 211 (pp.205-7)

Christopher remains in the luggage rack until the train reaches its final stop. He evades the policemen looking for him and follows his imaginary red line off the platform and out into the main hall of the station. Here Christopher is again overwhelmed by an information overload. He illustrates this through a paragraph listing all the signs and notices, followed by the same paragraph all jumbled up. He is frightened and confused, and wards off a man who approaches him by taking out his Swiss Army Knife.

When Christopher finds the tube station to get him to Willesden Junction, he watches other people use the ticket machine until he understands what to do. He says the escalators make him feel like he's in 'a science fiction film about the future' (p.212), showing how little knowledge Christopher has of worldly realities. By the time he gets to the underground platform he is very sick, confused and frightened. The crowds of people make him feel uneasy and the approaching trains sound 'like people fighting with swords' (p.216), so he sits groaning to himself. The chapter ends with a long sentence evoking his state of confusion and anxiety:

> And it was exactly like having flu that time because I wanted it to stop, like you can just pull the plug of a computer out of the wall if it crashes, because I wanted to go to sleep so that I wouldn't have to think because the only thing I could think was how much it hurt because there was no room for anything else in my head, but I couldn't go to sleep and I just had to sit there and there was nothing to do except to wait and to hurt (p.217).

Chapter 223 (Inter-chapter) (pp.218-20)

Christopher describes an advertisement in the tube station for holidays in Malaysia. Once again he points out that, unlike most people, he doesn't find going to new places relaxing.

Chapter 227 (pp.221-41)

Christopher sits in the train station with his eyes closed for 'approximately 5 hours' (p.221) listening to the rhythm of the trains coming and going. When he finally looks at his watch it is 8.07 pm. He notices that Toby has gone missing, but he also notices the screens that announce when the trains are coming, which he finds reassuring because he knows what will happen (p.223). He finds Toby on the tracks and climbs down to try to catch him. A man with diamond pattern socks yells at him to get off the tracks, but Christopher is only concerned with catching Toby, so that when the train comes the man saves Christopher's life by pulling him clear. Christopher's rescuer and another woman try to help Christopher, but he screams when they touch him and he threatens them with his Swiss Army Knife.

Finally Christopher succeeds in catching the train to Willesden Junction, where he buys a map and finds the way to his mother's house. When his mother comes home she is in the middle of an argument with Mr Shears, a sign perhaps that their relationship is troubled. Interestingly, when Mr Shears calls her Judy (p.233) this is the first time in the novel we learn Christopher's mother's first name.

Not surprisingly, Christopher's mother's first reaction to seeing Christopher after two years is to put her arms around him, and of course Christopher pushes her away, so hard that he falls over (p.233). A little later, she asks Christopher if "just for once" he will let her hold his hand, but he simply says "I don't like people holding my hand" (p.237). Christopher's dislike of human contact, and his inability to understand or respond to other people's emotional needs, seems perfectly reasonable to himself. However, most readers will feel sympathy for his mother in these scenes, because even in the highly emotional moment of being reunited with her son he is unable to express affection for her and will not let her express affection for him.

When Christopher turns up Mr Shears is clearly on edge, and Christopher feels wary of him. Christopher and his mother talk, and when Christopher tells her that he thought she was dead she makes 'a loud wailing noise like an animal on a nature programme on television' (p.236), a sound that unnerves Christopher because he doesn't know what it means.

A policeman visits the flat to check that Christopher is happy to stay in London, but at 2.31 am Christopher's father arrives and argues with

Christopher's mother. Christopher overhears them as they shout accusations at each other about failing Christopher as parents: Christopher's father by lying to him, Christopher's mother by leaving without any explanation.

Christopher's father comes into his room, but Christopher is frightened of him and clutches his Swiss Army Knife. When his father holds up his outspread fingers, Christopher refuses to respond. The policeman returns and Christopher's father is forced to leave.

This is a highly emotional, even tragic scene, but it is told in a factual, unemotional way. Christopher's father has certainly been the better parent over the last two years, taking full responsibility for Christopher's welfare. However, because of the lie he has told, he has lost Christopher's trust completely, and the remainder of the novel shows his efforts to repair this relationship.

Chapter 229 (Inter-chapter) (pp.242-4)

Christopher describes one of his favourite dreams, in which he imagines a virus that is spread by facial expressions so that 'eventually there is no one left in the world except people who don't look at other people's faces' (p.242). This fantasy doesn't even include the people who are closest to him, like his parents and Siobhan. It seems that in Christopher's ideal world he is completely and utterly alone.

Chapter 233 (pp.245-68)

The final chapter of the novel is also the longest. Things move very quickly in this chapter, giving a sense of what the earlier part of the novel might have been like without the inter-chapters that pace the narrative.

Christopher stays for a short time with his mother and Mr Shears, although Mr Shears is clearly unhappy about having Christopher in the house. We see examples of Christopher's behavioural problems, like throwing a tantrum in the supermarket and wandering off at night, and we see his mother's attempts to deal with him patiently while she is under a lot of pressure both from Mr Shears and from Christopher's father. Significantly, Christopher has no sympathy for her difficulties and he continues to badger her about his Maths A level exam, which makes her increasingly exasperated. She tells him that he will have to sit the exam next year, and in response he stops sleeping and eating.

Over the next few days, Christopher's mother and Mr Shears start arguing about what to do with Christopher, until one night Mr Shears drunkenly yells at Christopher: "You think you're so fucking clever, don't you? Don't you ever, ever think about other people for one second, eh?" (p.252). This shows how people tend to interpret Christopher's behaviour as selfishness rather than a medical condition. It also shows how looking after Christopher can strain relationships. The following morning, Christopher's mother takes Mr Shears's car and they return to the house in Swindon. Christopher's father agrees to move out and let them stay at his house until they can get a place on their own.

Although Christopher's mother doesn't appreciate the importance of the Maths A level to him, when Christopher goes back to school Siobhan immediately agrees to make the arrangements. Over the next few days Christopher sits his three A level papers, even though he has hardly slept or eaten for several days.

After the exam is finished, Christopher's father comes round to ask how he went, and tells him, "I'm very proud of you, Christopher" (p.261). But he also tells Christopher's mother that she has to find somewhere else to live. She gets a new job, starts taking medication, and she and Christopher move into a new flat where Christopher has to share a bathroom. This is a very difficult time for Christopher – 'there were more bad things than good things' (p.263). His pet rat, Toby, dies and he doesn't like waiting for his exam results, but he shows some signs of growing maturity by helping his mother paint her room. When Christopher stays at his father's house he barricades himself in his room and refuses to speak to his father, even through the closed door.

Eventually, Christopher's father finds a way to re-establish their relationship. Showing Christopher a kitchen timer, he gets Christopher to agree to listen to him for five minutes. He says that Christopher's refusal to talk to him "hurts too much", and that restoring their relationship is "more important than anything else" (p.265). Putting it in terms that appeal to Christopher, he calls it "A project we have to do together. You have to spend more time with me. And I…I have to show you that you can trust me" (p.265). Christopher's father then gives him a dog, which he will be able to visit at his father's house.

Christopher gets an A grade in his Maths A level, which makes him happy. His mother falls ill with the flu so he stays for three days with his father and, although he is still scared, he is reassured by the presence of his dog.

The novel ends on a note of triumph. Christopher looks forward to doing A level Further Maths the next year, then eventually going to university, getting a First Class Honours Degree and becoming a scientist:

> And I know I can do this because I went to London on my own, and because I solved the mystery of Who Killed Wellington? and I found my mother and I was brave and I wrote a book and that means I can do anything (p.268).

There is ambivalence about this optimism, however, because Christopher is still living in his own private world, indifferent to his parents' emotional struggles. He shows a new-found confidence in dealing with his condition, but is still not capable of understanding and empathising with the emotional lives of others.

Appendix (pp.269-72)

Christopher gives the solution to his favourite question from the Maths A level exam. This is an unusual way to end a novel, but underlines the fact that Christopher's primary interest is still with mathematical and logical problems rather than his relationships with other people.

CHARACTERS & RELATIONSHIPS

Christopher Boone

Key quotes

'I find people confusing' (p.19).

'I do not tell lies...But it is not because I am a good person. It is because I can't tell lies' (p.24).

'A white lie is not a lie at all' (p.62).

'I solved the mystery of Who Killed Wellington? and I found my mother and I was brave and I wrote a book and that means I can do anything' (p.268).

Christopher Boone is both the narrator and the protagonist of the novel: almost everything is described in Christopher's words and from Christopher's point of view, so that readers 'see' the world through Christopher's eyes. His 'Behavioural Problems' (p.59) mean that he finds it difficult to relate to people on an emotional level, so although readers learn a great deal about Christopher they learn much less about the other characters.

Christopher writes the book as a record of his investigation into the murder of the dog Wellington. However, his investigation reaches a crisis when he discovers that his mother is alive and his father has lied to him.

Overwhelmed by this information, Christopher goes into a state of shock. This is soon followed by a state of panic when his father admits that he killed Wellington and Christopher starts to fear his father might try to kill him. Christopher's journey to London is a test of all his reserves of courage and ingenuity, but is ultimately rewarding because he is reunited with his mother and he discovers a new confidence in overcoming some aspects of his condition.

Although his investigation uncovers his parents' lies and betrayals, and stirs up extreme emotions in his parents of anger, bitterness and regret, Christopher is unaffected by these crises, caring only about his maths exam.

Key point

The book gives us an insight into Christopher's emotionally simple world, challenging our ordinary expectations of character and personality. Christopher's unusual perspective on life is partly a result of Asperger's Syndrome and partly just an expression of his unique personality as a human being.

The next four sections consider four aspects of Christopher's character that influence how he sees and responds to the world. The last two sections consider Christopher as a detective and as a writer.

Emotional Detachment

Christopher he says he finds people confusing because they 'do a lot of talking without using any words' (p.19). Christopher is unable to 'read' other people's emotions by interpreting non-verbal signs such as facial expressions, gestures and tone of voice. When Christopher's father discovers his notebook, Christopher says 'I didn't realise he was angry because he wasn't shouting' (p.101). Christopher also doesn't like being touched, and feels no desire to express affection for other people; for instance, he pushes his mother away when she tries to hug him after not seeing him for two years (p.233).

Information Overload

Christopher is proud of his powers of observation and memory. He explains that 'My memory is like a film' (p.96), and later he boasts that 'I see everything' (p.174), proving it by giving a minutely detailed description of a field. But this can be a disadvantage, because in unfamiliar situations Christopher experiences 'information overload'. The first example occurs when a policeman starts asking him questions: 'They were stacking up in my head like loaves in the factory where Uncle Terry works' (p.8). At these times he starts 'groaning', the noise he makes 'when there is too much information coming into my head from the outside world' (p.8). We see this problem most clearly on the trip to London, when Christopher illustrates with two successive paragraphs how all the signs in the railway station become jumbled and confused (pp.208-9).

The Need for Order

Because of his sensitivity to information overload, Christopher doesn't like new places or unfamiliar situations. He has a strong need for order and regularity in his life and for this reason develops a number of odd habits. For instance, he doesn't like eating or touching things that are yellow or brown. Although he admits that this is 'sort of being silly', he goes on to explain that 'in life you have to take lots of decisions...So it is good to have a reason why you hate some things and you like others' (pp.106-7). Christopher explains to the school psychologist, Mr Jeavons, that his system of Good Days and Black Days, based on how many red or yellow cars he sees, is just a way of 'putting things in a nice order' (p.31).

Another aspect of Christopher's need for order is his need always to know the time. The novel begins with the words 'It was 7 minutes after midnight' (p.1), and throughout the novel Christopher repeatedly gives the exact time when things happen. At the police station he screams when they try to take his watch from him 'because I needed to know exactly what time it was' (p.17). Later he gives an example of his daily timetable: 'I like timetables because I like to know when everything is going to happen' (p.192).

Science and Mathematics

Christopher's love of order explains his passion for mathematics, which is based entirely on logic and doesn't involve ambiguity or emotional judgment. Christopher calms himself by doing maths calculations in his head, such as doubling twos (p.149) or solving quadratic equations (p.201). He even expresses his dilemma of needing to run away from his father but being afraid of new places in terms of a mathematical equation (p.168).

However, Christopher is also keen to show that mathematics is not as cut-and-dried as some people think. He discusses the complexities of prime numbers, which he thinks are 'like life' (p.15) because they do not obey any pattern, and he shows how the formula for predicting the population of frogs in the school pond can produce chaotic results, so that a whole population can suddenly become extinct 'just because that is the way the numbers work' (p.128).

Christopher as a Detective

Christopher is a fan of Sherlock Holmes, but it is doubtful whether Christopher makes a good detective. Solving a mystery involves at least three processes: gathering information, sifting out what is important and making connections.

Christopher is certainly highly observant, but this is different from being perceptive and there are many clues that Christopher misses because of his lack of understanding of other people's emotions. Moreover, a lot of what Christopher observes is irrelevant detail. As we see in the train station, Christopher finds it difficult to 'process' information; he 'sees everything' but can't mentally 'edit out' what is not important.

The third challenge is to put the clues together. Christopher insists on the importance of this in his conversation with Mr Jeavons:

> I was just noticing how things were and that wasn't clever. That was just being observant. Being clever was when you looked at how things were and used the evidence to work out something new (p.32).

Christopher does his best to work out who killed Wellington using a 'Chain of Reasoning' based on the information he has available (p.54). But because he doesn't appreciate the importance of certain clues – that his father had an affair with Mrs Shears but "she's not a friend any more" (p.63) – Christopher is completely taken by surprise when his father confesses. Christopher boasts at the end of the novel that 'I solved the mystery of Who Killed Wellington?' (p.268), but we should remember that he didn't really work it out on his own.

Christopher as a Writer

The Curious Incident... can be seen as a story about the growth of a writer. Of course, Christopher is a fictional character and a real-life Christopher couldn't or wouldn't have written such a novel. But, through his narrator, Christopher Boone, Mark Haddon shows how the process of writing a story can itself be a journey of discovery and an immensely fulfilling experience.

Christopher's writing is not a solitary process, but is initiated and guided by Siobhan, who rightly sees it as a 'project' that will have a number of benefits for Christopher. It is Siobhan who first suggests what to write about, and she helps 'with the spelling and the footnotes' (p.34). Christopher writes a murder mystery because Siobhan advises him to write 'something I would want to read myself' (p.5). Siobhan also helps with other suggestions, such as how to describe people by mentioning one or two details 'so that people could make a picture of them in their head' (p.85). Most importantly, she helps Christopher stick to things that will be of interest to the reader.

In general, however, Siobhan lets Christopher tell his story in his own way. This means including chapters on topics that interest him, such as the Milky Way galaxy (pp.11-12) and the constellation Orion (pp.156-7). But, as the story progresses the narrative chapters get longer and more complex, while the digressions are reduced to brief interludes. We might see this as a sign that Christopher is developing his skill as a storyteller.

Christopher says he doesn't like 'proper novels' because 'they are lies about things which didn't happen' (p.25), and because they contain baffling metaphorical passages like 'I am veined with iron, with silver and with streaks of common mud' (p.5). This example of ridiculously 'purple prose' can be seen as Mark Haddon's joke at the expense of extravagantly 'literary' language.

Christopher's writing style is seemingly unsophisticated; most of his sentences are short, factual statements. However, sometimes Christopher writes longer sentences in which a string of phrases is joined together by conjunctions ('and', 'or', 'but', 'because'). For example, when he describes the meaning of breathing out loudly through your nose, he writes:

> it all depends on how much air comes out of your nose and how fast and what shape your mouth is when you do it and how you are sitting and what you just said before and hundreds of other things which are too complicated to work out in a few seconds (p.19).

This passage uses language very effectively to imitate the overwhelming rush of information that causes Christopher distress. There are many such passages scattered through the novel. Through using Christopher as a narrator, Mark Haddon shows that even someone with seemingly limited linguistic resources can be a highly engaging and effective writer.

Ed Boone (Christopher's Father)

Key quotes

'Father...always tells me the truth, which means that he loves me' (p.109).
"I did it for your good, Christopher. Honestly I did. I never meant to lie" (p.143).
"It's bloody hard telling the truth all the time. Sometimes it's impossible" (p.150).
"This just hurts too much...You have to learn to trust me...This s more important than anything else" (p.265).

In some ways Ed Boone is the tragic figure at the centre of the novel. His emotional crisis is the catalyst for the events that Christopher describes. Two years before the beginning of the narrative his wife left him and he began having an affair with his neighbour Mrs Shears. He is ordinarily a gentle and patient man, but when that relationship broke down he killed Mrs Shears's dog in a fit of rage: "it was like everything I'd been bottling up for two years just..." (p.152).

Ed Boone is a loving father who does his best to look after a demanding son. In some ways he can be seen as a positive role model, because single fathers are relatively unusual in fiction and Ed Boone does an excellent job of coping with Christopher's needs. As he makes clear in his argument with Christopher's mother (p.240), he is the one who cooks Christopher's meals (which involves dealing with Christopher's odd eating habits), washes Christopher's clothes, looks after him on weekends (for instance, by taking Christopher to the zoo in Chapter 137) and when he is sick or gets into fights.

This level of commitment is clear right at the beginning of the novel, when Ed collects Christopher at the police station. Christopher overhears his father shouting, and we can infer that this is not the first time he has had to intervene when his son has been in trouble, particularly with strangers who do not understand his condition. However, because his son is not capable of providing him with affectionate companionship, Ed Boone is rather lonely. Apart from his affair with Mrs Shears, which ends before the novel begins, his only friend seems to be his employee, Rhodri. He runs a small business repairing heaters and, while he is able to provide for himself and his son, he is not wealthy.

Ed Boone's tragedy arises out of the lie he tells his son. When Christopher's mother leaves him for Mr Shears, Ed tells Christopher that she has gone to hospital. Later he tells Christopher that he had lied because he "didn't know how to explain" (p.144). This important scene is first related from Christopher's point of view in the flashback chapters (43 and 53) where Christopher discusses his mother's death. Christopher's father begins by saying, "I'm afraid you won't be seeing your mother for a while" but doesn't look at his son (p.28). Ironically, Christopher enjoys this because he doesn't like people looking at him when they talk to him, but Ed's behaviour indicates to the reader that he is not telling Christopher the truth.

When Ed Boone finds Christopher reading the letters, he bursts into tears and tries to explain: "I did it for your good, Christopher" (p.143). However, it is difficult to see how it is better for Christopher to think his mother is dead. The real reasons for Ed Boone's lie are self-centred. He will find it easier to get over Mrs Boone leaving him if he never has to see her or talk to her again, and he will be able to punish her by denying her access to her son. But this raises the question of why Mrs Shears, who knows about her husband's relationship with Judy Boone, goes along with the lie and doesn't tell Christopher the truth. Clearly, they both find it more convenient to take advantage of Christopher's innocence.

Apart from the one big mistake he makes, Ed Boone is a good father to Christopher. Significantly, he understands how important the Maths A level exam is to Christopher. He confronts Mrs Gascoyne at the school, insisting that they make the arrangements because "this is the one thing he is really good at" (p.57). At the end of the novel, too, he shows his sensitivity by proposing that he and Christopher work on their relationship together as a project, and he buys Christopher a dog because he knows Christopher loves dogs. Ed Boone's emotional crisis leads him to make mistakes, but his efforts to redeem himself win the reader's sympathy, even if he receives no sympathy from Christopher.

Judy Boone (Christopher's Mother)

Key quotes

'I was not a very good mother, Christopher. Maybe if things had been differant, maybe if you'd been differant, I might have been better at it' (p.133).

'Your father is a much more pacient person...But that's not the way I am and there's nothing I can do to change that' (p.133).

'I thought that what I was doing was the best for all of us' (p.137).

Given that Christopher's mother doesn't actually appear in the novel until near the end (p.233), we don't get to know her very well. Even then, because we see things from Christopher's point of view, the narrative provides little information about her thoughts and feelings. As readers, we have to do a little detective work to piece her together as a character.

We learn most about Judy Boone from the letters she writes to Christopher, especially the longest of these where she explains why she left. She admits that she was not a very good mother and lacked the patience to deal with Christopher's condition. But she sees herself as incapable of changing: 'there's nothing I can do to change that' (p.133). She also sees Christopher as incapable of changing: 'maybe if you'd been differant, I might have been better at it' (p.133). This suggests that she is inclined to be pessimistic, and when Christopher states near the end of the novel that 'the doctor gave her pills to take every morning to stop her feeling sad' (p.262) we might guess that she suffers from depression, which would explain why she finds it difficult to cope with such a demanding son.

The fact that she left Christopher without saying goodbye suggests that she is someone who acts on sudden emotional impulses rather than thinking through her actions. This is confirmed later, on the morning after Mr Shears verbally abuses Christopher, when without telling Mr Shears she packs up her clothes and drives back to Swindon with Christopher in Mr Shears's car (p.252).

Other details give clues to her character, such as when Christopher tells us that she used to say to him "If I hadn't married your father I think I'd be living in a little farmhouse in the South of France with someone called Jean" (p.98). When Mr Shears retrieves his car, the books that he throws onto the lawn are *Diana: Her True Story* by Andrew Morton and *Rivals* by Jilly Cooper, an author of steamy romance novels (p.259). These clues indicate that Judy Boone is inclined to romantic daydreams, due to feeling unhappy and unfulfilled in her life.

At the end of the novel, she appears to be making an effort to deal with her problems. She is unable to appreciate how important Christopher's maths exam is to him, and finds dealing with his insistence on doing his Maths A level too stressful on top of everything else. But she manages to cope with Christopher's tantrum in the shopping centre without losing her temper (pp.245-6), and she sees a doctor to get medication to help with her depression. She also does some of the things associated with 'turning over a new leaf', like getting a new job, finding a new place to live and painting her room. These signs indicate that, despite the opinion she expresses in her letters, she may be capable of changing and learning how to live with Christopher better.

Siobhan (Pronounced shi-VAUN)

Siobhan is Christopher's favourite teacher and is, perhaps, the person who understands him best. She helps him in many ways: she teaches him techniques for coping with stressful situations; she gives him the idea of writing a book about his investigation; she gives him advice on how to do descriptions and helps him focus on what readers are likely to find interesting. She does more than just 'help with the spelling and the grammar and the footnotes' (p.34). In the end it is Siobhan who arranges for Christopher to sit his Maths A level exam (p.256).

Mrs Alexander

Mrs Alexander is an important character because she is the first person Christopher forms a relationship with independently of his family and his school. He decides she is a good person because she likes dogs and because she wears New Balance trainers with red laces (p.50). She has a knack for drawing Christopher out in conversation, and encourages his awkward attempts to 'do chatting'. It is from Mrs Alexander that Christopher learns that his mother and Mr Shears were 'doing sex' (p.76), although Christopher doesn't know what to make of this information.

Relationships: Responsibilities of Parents and Children

When Ed Boone arrives at Mr Shears's flat in London, he and Judy Boone accuse each other of failing Christopher as parents:

> And Mother shouted, "What in God's name did you think you were playing at, saying those things to him?"
> And Father shouted, "What was I playing at? You were the one that bloody left" (p.239).

Judy Boone seems to have the greatest difficulty with Christopher. As we learn from her letters, she would lose her temper when he had screaming fits in public and could not accept his refusal to eat. Ed Boone seems more easygoing, but their differences of opinion about how to deal with Christopher's condition lead to the breakdown of their marriage.

When she starts seeing Mr Shears, Judy Boone initially refuses to move in with him because of Christopher. However, after she breaks her toes and sees how well Christopher and his father get along without her, she begins to feel sorry for herself: 'I realised you and your father were probably better off if I wasn't living in the house' (p.136). Where she really lets Christopher down is not so much by going to London with Mr Shears, but by failing to tell Christopher. She finds the task of explaining her emotional decisions to her logical and unemotional son too difficult to contemplate. Judy Boone faithfully writes to Christopher every week, but the fact that in two years she doesn't make the relatively easy journey from London to Swindon to see him suggests that she would rather leave the difficulties of dealing with Christopher to his father.

Ed Boone also lets Christopher down by failing to explain the breakdown in his relationship with Christopher's mother. Given that their arguments cause Christopher emotional distress, it seems that Christopher would have been capable of understanding why his mother decided to leave. However, Christopher's father takes the 'easy way out' by pretending to Christopher that she is dead. In other words, he fails to respect Christopher's ability to understand the situation and his right to know the truth.

Key point

Christopher is aware that his condition puts a lot of strain on his parents: 'I used to think that Mother and Father might get divorced…This was because of the stress of looking after someone who has Behavioural Problems like I have' (p.59). In the course of the novel, however, Christopher discovers that he is far more capable than he realised of controlling his behaviour and dealing with his fears. Ironically, it is only when both his parents fail him that he is forced to make this discovery.

In other words, Christopher learns to some extent to take responsibility for his condition. It seems like a setback, therefore, when Christopher has a panic attack in the shopping centre (pp.245-6). Clearly it will be a long process, but by helping his mother paint her room and his father to tend the garden he seems to be making a genuine effort to have a better, more reciprocal, less dependent relationship with his parents.

Relationships: Teacher and Pupil

Christopher's relationship with Siobhan is perhaps the most positive relationship in the novel. She helps him write the book, an achievement that enormously boosts his self-confidence. She also teaches him techniques for dealing with his panic attacks and for controlling some of his fears. In addition, she appreciates the importance of his maths exam. Mathematics may not be, as his father says, "the one thing he is really good at" (p.57), but it is Christopher's greatest passion and source of pride. Siobhan's arranging for him to sit the three papers ensures the novel's 'happy ending', reinforcing the life-enhancing possibilities of a strong relationship between teacher and pupil.

Relationships: Husbands and Wives

One of the sad things about *The Curious Incident…* (although it doesn't make Christopher sad, of course) is that there are no couples who have healthy, trusting relationships. The marriages of both the Shearses and the Boones have broken down before the novel begins. We do not know about the Shearses, but the Boones' marriage ends because of their differences of opinion about how to deal with Christopher's behavioural problems, and we know that Christopher is aware of these tensions (p.59).

In the middle of the novel, when Ed Boone tries to explain to Christopher how he came to kill Wellington, he gives an insight into why his relationship with Mrs Shears broke down:

> I think she cared more for that bloody dog than for me, for us. And maybe that's not so stupid, looking back. Maybe we are a bloody handful...I mean, shit, buddy, we're not exactly low-maintenance are we…? (p.151).

There are signs that Mrs Shears, like most people, finds Christopher's behavioural problems 'a bloody handful', such as when she moves the furniture to vacuum their living room: 'Mrs Shears did the hoovering once but I did groaning and she shouted at Father and she never did it again' (p.60). However, it is not just Christopher's fault that this relationship ends: Ed admits that he, too, is 'a bloody handful', although we can only guess what he means by this.

Similarly, the relationship between Judy Boone and Mr Shears seems to break down under the pressure of dealing with Christopher. Mr Shears is hostile to Christopher's presence right from the beginning and is only willing to allow him to stay "for a few days" (p.245). He is very offended when Christopher rejects the books he brings back from the library (p.251), judging Christopher's insensitivity to be ingratitude rather than an aspect of his condition. When Mr Shears comes into Christopher's room when he is drunk, he says, "Don't you ever, ever think about other people for one second, eh?" (p.252). The next day, Judy Boone heads back to Swindon and the relationship is over. However, we should remember that she and Mr Shears are arguing when Christopher first meets them in London, so he is not the only cause of their break-up.

Of the other main characters, Mrs Alexander lives happily alone with her dog, and Christopher doesn't mention if Siobhan has a partner. The novel, therefore, paints a rather bleak picture of relationships. Each of the four relationships between the Shearses and the Boones disintegrates into arguments and estrangement. Everyone has trouble maintaining honest, loving, reciprocal relationships, throwing Christopher's problems into sharp relief.

THEMES & ISSUES

Truth, Lies and Trust

Key quotes

'[H]e always tells me the truth, which means that he loves me' (p.109).

'Father had murdered Wellington. That meant he could murder me, because I couldn't trust him, even though he had said, 'Trust me,' because he had told a lie about a big thing' (pp.152-3).

The central drama of *The Curious Incident...* is the deterioration and then restoration of the relationship between Christopher and his father, in which the interplay between truth, lies and trust is crucial. Christopher announces quite early in the novel that he 'can't tell lies' (p.24) because thinking about things that didn't happen makes him feel 'shaky and scared' (p.25). Christopher also explains that he finds people confusing because he cannot interpret their facial expressions, and he finds jokes and metaphors confusing because he does not like it when words can have several meanings. Christopher has a very literal approach to language and to people: he interprets everything people say literally, and he always says exactly what he means.

Because of his somewhat simplistic attitude to language and communication, Christopher is vulnerable to being lied to. He avoids strangers because he finds it difficult to interpret their words and their facial expressions, and he trusts blindly in the people who are close to him, relying on them always to tell him the truth.

But when Christopher says, 'I can't tell lies', this does not mean that he always tells the truth. Firstly, he often isn't able to piece together the truth, particularly where it concerns other people and their relationships. Secondly, in his discussion of white lies, he shows that he is capable of being deceitful. He cleverly argues that 'everything you say is a white lie' (p.62) because you never tell the whole truth about everything, but this is not the real reason why he tells a white lie: 'I said a white lie because I knew that Father didn't want me to be a detective' (p.62).

In an important later scene (Chapter 127), Christopher and his father have a scuffle after his father discovers Christopher's notebook. His father is angry because Christopher has once again broken his promise by continuing his investigation. Christopher uses some ingenious 'reasoning' (p.72) to argue that asking Mrs Alexander about Mr Shears is 'like chatting' and doesn't break the literal interpretation of the promise, even though it goes against its spirit. Christopher's father has read the book, though, and is well aware of Christopher's thought process, asserting that: "You knew exactly what you were doing" (p.102).

The following day, during their visit to Twycross Zoo (Chapter 137), Christopher's father apologises for becoming angry with him. He asks, "Christopher, you do understand that I love you?" Christopher's reply is important:

> I said, 'Yes,' because loving someone is helping them when they get into trouble, and looking after them, and telling them the truth, and Father looks after me when I get into trouble...and he always tells me the truth, which means that he loves me (p.109).

In the course of the novel, Christopher learns that things are not so simple, and that his father loves him even though he lied to him. But Christopher's initial response to finding out that his father killed Wellington and lied about Christopher's mother being dead is an extreme reaction:

> Father had murdered Wellington. That meant he could murder me, because I couldn't trust him, even though he had said, 'Trust me,' because he had told a lie about a big thing (p.153).

Part of Christopher's 'project' (p.265) in learning to trust his father again involves understanding that his father was right when he said, "It's bloody hard telling the truth all the time. Sometimes it's impossible" (p.150). However, an important aspect of Christopher's character is his lack of self-consciousness: he doesn't seem to reflect on his own actions or motives. He finds ingenious arguments to justify his white lies, and seemingly won't admit that continuing his investigation behind his father's back is a form of deceit, equivalent to a lie.

In order to reach a level of maturity in his understanding of truth, lies and trust, Christopher needs to accept that everyone, even himself, is capable of dishonesty, particularly in times of emotional stress. There is no simple equation between loving someone and always telling them the truth. Learning to trust his father again will involve Christopher learning to trust less blindly, in an awareness of the difficulty of always being honest.

Disability and Independence

Key quote

'And I know I can do this because I went to London on my own...and I found my mother and I was brave and I wrote a book and that means I can do anything' (p.268).

Christopher knows that he has 'Behavioural Problems', and he knows that looking after him causes his parents a great deal of stress (p.59). But he doesn't think of himself as someone with a disability. He says, 'I'm not a spazzer' (p.33), and asserts that 'All the other children at my school are stupid' (p.56), showing that he can be just as insensitive about disabled people as anyone else. Christopher is never ashamed of his condition but, on the contrary, is proud of and even a little arrogant about his unusual abilities, like his photographic memory and his skill with numbers.

Christopher knows that some of his behaviour and habits may seem strange to 'normal' people, but he also shows how strange normal people are. For instance, when the psychologist suggests that Christopher's system of Good Days and Bad Days based on red and yellow cars is illogical, Christopher replies that it is just as illogical for people who work in offices to let their mood be affected by the weather (p.31). He also argues that it is illogical for normal people to get upset about things that didn't happen, or to worry about silly things like whether they left the gas cooker on (p.178).

During the course of the novel Christopher punches a policeman, has a fist fight with his father, brandishes his knife at several people and has screaming fits, but he feels no guilt and is never apologetic about his behaviour. So, we can understand why his parents find Christopher infuriating – he seems never to take responsibility for anything. Indeed, one of the most interesting aspects of Christopher's growth through the novel is the way his journey to London forces him to become independent and take responsibility for his actions.

Key point

Christopher's journey is not just a story about overcoming disability: it is a journey taken by all adolescents as they learn to stand on their own two feet, take on challenges and deal with the consequences of their mistakes.

Through this journey Christopher learns that perhaps his 'Behavioural Problems' do not limit him as much as he thought, and that some aspects of his condition have more to do with ingrained habits of thinking – 'I can't do that' – rather than real inability. For someone who has never been beyond the end of the street on their own, making the trip to London is a huge achievement and is, in a sense, a journey of liberation. It frees Christopher from the idea that, because he has a disability, the range of options available to him must be limited. It gives him the confidence to dream about one day going to university and becoming a scientist, an ambition that would have been merely a daydream for someone frightened to go past the end of the street.

However, although Christopher learns to overcome his fears, at the end of the novel he still does not seem any more sensitive to other people's emotions than at the beginning. For instance, he pushes his mother away when she tries to hug him, and won't even let her hold his hand (p.237). He stubbornly insists on sitting his maths exam, even when it is clear she is stressed and upset. And he doesn't seem to understand or have any sympathy for his father's grief and pain, although in the end he does agree to the project to rebuild trust between them.

Therefore, *The Curious Incident...* doesn't offer any miracles. Christopher's trip to London is a significant achievement in terms of learning coping skills and independence, and in terms of overcoming fears associated with his disability. However, the novel also shows the limits to Christopher's improvement: he is still emotionally detached from his parents and, although the scenes where he helps them with chores suggest the beginnings of a more reciprocal relationship, there is still a long way to go.

Reason and Emotion

Key quotes

'[I]ntuition can sometimes get things wrong...And intuition is what people use in life to make decisions. But logic can help you work out the right answer' (p.82).

'And this shows that sometimes people want to be stupid and they do not want to know the truth' (p.113).

Christopher is highly self-aware about his condition. He knows he has a very logical mind and that he has difficulty understanding other people's emotions. He also knows that people will be critical of his emotional detachment, seeing him as cold and heartless because they think that it is our emotions that make us human. Throughout the novel, Christopher raises a number of issues concerning the relationship between reason and emotion. On one level, Christopher is simply trying to describe his own view of the world. But, on another level, he is engaging in a complex debate about the nature of human consciousness and personality.

Emotions Make People Illogical

Christopher is highly critical of the way people allow their emotions to override their logical thinking. For instance, although Christopher likes Sherlock Holmes, he doesn't like the author of the Sherlock Holmes stories, Sir Arthur Conan Doyle, because he believed in the supernatural. According to Christopher, the reason Doyle thought you could communicate with the dead 'was because his son died of influenza during the First World War and he still wanted to talk to him' (p.111). So, too, Doyle believed the photograph of the Cottingley Fairies was real, which to Christopher was 'being stupid' because 'the fairies look just like fairies in old books… which is like aliens landing on the earth and being like Daleks from Doctor Who' (p.112). For Christopher this shows that 'sometimes people want to be stupid and they do not want to know the truth' (p.113). Christopher can't understand how a person's emotional need for things to be true can override their logical thinking. But Christopher, too, is capable of self-deception: at the end he claims to have solved the mystery of who killed Wellington (p.268). This is not true, but we can understand Christopher's emotional need to believe it.

Christopher argues with Reverend Peters about the existence of heaven (pp.42-3), asserting with his characteristic bluntness that 'when Mother died she didn't go to heaven because heaven doesn't exist' (p.42). When Reverend Peters claims that heaven is "not in our universe", Christopher argues that such a thing would only be possible if dead people passed through a black hole, and 'dead people would have to be fired into space on rockets to get there, and they aren't, or people would notice' (p.42). Still, Christopher likes to think that there are 'molecules of Mother' in the atmosphere (p.44), indicating that, in his own scientific way, Christopher is capable of using logic to satisfy an emotional need.

Emotions Cause Unnecessary Suffering

Christopher is critical of the way people allow regrets about the past or anxieties about the future to upset them. In the chapter where he explains how his memory works, he says that 'other people have pictures in their head of things which aren't real and didn't happen' (p.98). He gives as examples his mother's daydream about living in the south of France and Siobhan's daydream about living in Cape Cod. For Christopher, imagining what might have been, like wondering what his mother would say if she was alive, is 'stupid because Mother is dead and you can't say anything to people who are dead and dead people can't think' (p.99). Therefore, when Siobhan asks Christopher if he is upset by the news that his mother was having an affair with Mr Shears, he says no, because "I would be feeling sad about something that isn't real and doesn't exist. And that would be stupid" (p.95).

Intuition Gets Things Wrong

Christopher is highly critical of intuition, using the example of the Monty Hall Problem to show that 'intuition can sometimes get things wrong…But logic can help you work out the right answer' (p.82).

However, Christopher's lack of intuition leads him to make mistakes. He doesn't suspect that his father was having an affair with Mrs Shears, and he doesn't suspect the real reason why his father tells him to stop his investigation. Therefore, when Christopher develops his 'Chain of Reasoning' to identify his 'Prime Suspect' (pp.53-5), he is rigorously logical but his lack of intuition means he isn't able to come up with the right answer. Important decisions in life, like detective work, often require a combination of intuition and logic, and need to deal with uncertainty and ambiguity as much as with definite facts.

The Mind is Like a Computer

Several times in the novel, Christopher compares his mind to a computer. He describes his groaning as 'like pressing CTRL + ALT + DEL and shutting down programs and turning the computer off and rebooting' (p.178). In Chapter 163, he develops an extended argument as to why 'the mind is just a complicated machine' (p.146). He tries to explain emotions as a mental process that is comparable to a computer process:

> people think they're not computers because they have feelings and computers don't have feelings. But feelings are just having a picture on the screen in your head…if it is a happy picture they smile and if it is a sad picture they cry (p.148).

This is a rather simplistic explanation of emotions, which are far more complex and unpredictable than Christopher's theory suggests. On one hand, this passage indicates that, in his own logical way, Christopher is trying to understand how emotions work. On the other hand, Christopher knows that people think emotions are what make them human, and that he himself might be seen as less 'human' because of his emotional disconnectedness. By giving a logical, scientific explanation of emotions, Christopher argues that emotions are not so special and that he is no less human for not feeling them.

Maths can be Unpredictable

Christopher tries to show that mathematics is more complex than many people realise. He objects to Mr Jeavons's opinion that 'maths wasn't like life because in life there are no straightforward answers at the end' (p.78). Christopher discusses the Monty Hall Problem to demonstrate this, but what the Monty Hall Problem really shows is 'that intuition can sometimes get things wrong' and that 'logic can help you work out the right answer' (p.82). However, there are other examples that illustrate Christopher's point better, such as prime numbers, which are very logical but which demonstrate no pattern (p.15), and the formula describing animal populations, which can produce results that are chaotic and unpredictable (p.128). In these examples, Christopher shows that, even though people think maths is always safe, logical and predictable, some mathematical problems have no straightforward answers at the end.

Christopher's Emotional Life

All these examples show that Christopher is deeply interested in philosophical questions about how the mind works and the nature of human consciousness, emotion and personality. He is aware that people find his emotional detachment unsettling, and that some people will pass moral judgment on this aspect of his personality, seeing him as cold and unfeeling. Christopher is anxious to show on the one hand that emotions are often a cause of bad decisions and unnecessary suffering and, on the other hand, that he is capable of greater understanding than people give him credit for.

Key point

What we learn from reading the novel is that, even if he has little empathy for other people, Christopher does have an intense emotional life of his own. We see this in his reaction to the news that his mother is alive, and in the way he stops sleeping and eating when he thinks he won't be able to sit his maths exam. Ironically, although Christopher cannot empathise with others, he encourages the reader to empathise with him. Through this, rather than through his logical and scientific arguments, we come to see Christopher as a human being whose sufferings and achievements we can relate to.

Unhappy Families

Christopher says 'I used to think that Mother and Father might get divorced...because of the stress of looking after someone who has Behavioural Problems like I have' (p.59). However, what the novel shows is that both his parents have behavioural problems of their own which cause the family to fall apart. Christopher's mother is short-tempered and suffers from depression, which may be part of the reason why she decides to leave when she feels 'like you didn't really need me at all' (p.136). Christopher's father is more even-tempered, but bottles up his emotions of anger and hurt to the point where he 'cracks' and kills Mrs Shears's dog. If Ed and Judy Boone had a healthier, more honest relationship, perhaps they would have been better able to deal with the issues raised by Christopher's condition.

One of the most distressing aspects of Christopher's personality is that he seems incapable of feeling or expressing affection for his parents. A passage near the beginning of the novel highlights this important issue:

> [Father] held up his right hand and spread his fingers out in a fan. I held up my left hand and spread my fingers out in a fan and we made our fingers and thumbs touch each other. We do this because sometimes Father wants to give me a hug, but I do not like hugging people, so we do this instead, and it means that he loves me (p.21).

It is interesting that Christopher says 'he loves me' rather than 'I love him'. Although Christopher's father feels the need to hug his son and tell him he loves him, Christopher feels no such need. Similarly, near the end of the novel, when Christopher's mother tries to put her arms around him he pushes her violently away (p.233), and later will not even let her hold his hand (p.237). The emotional relationship between Christopher and his parents appears to be a one-way street. We begin to understand what Christopher's parents must experience: they love their son and need to show their affection for him, but he doesn't understand this need and rejects their attempts to physically express their affection.

This raises an interesting question: can Christopher really be said to 'love' his parents if he is incapable of emotional communication with them? There are various signs that he does love them. He misses his mother, and in his scientific way likes to imagine that her ashes have become part of the atmosphere (p.44). He appreciates his father's efforts to look after him, and in the early part of the novel Christopher and his father share a companionship that is clearly important to both of them. Most significantly, however, at the end of the novel Christopher agrees to his father's 'project' which means they will spend time together until Christopher can learn to trust him again (p.265). Christopher can't understand his father's emotions, that "this [separation] just hurts too much" (p.265), but he does agree to the project, indicating that the relationship with his father is important to him even though he does not express this in emotional terms.

The novel doesn't end with a reassuring picture of 'a happy family' reunited after all their troubles. Ed and Judy Boone do not get back together, but in the circumstances they do show a great degree of cooperation in looking after Christopher. In particular, Judy supports Ed's efforts to rebuild his relationship with his son, standing by to provide reassurance to Christopher when they have their important talk (p.265). Given that Ed Boone's lies effectively cut off communication between Christopher and his mother, her support for the rebuilding of Christopher's relationship with his father shows that they have managed to put the past behind them.

The Complexities of Language

Christopher Boone shows himself to be unusually aware of language. This interest reflects a theory about disorders such as Asperger's Syndrome: that they involve essentially linguistic problems, concerning the ways in which people such as Christopher understand and use language.

Non-verbal Communication

Christopher is aware of his problems with interpreting non-verbal forms of communication, such as facial expressions and gestures. He finds people confusing because 'people do a lot of talking without using any words' (p.19). Gestures such as raising one eyebrow or breathing out through your nose are ambiguous to Christopher because they can mean many different things, depending on context.

Ambiguity

The reason Christopher can't understand gestures is that he doesn't like ambiguity. He says, 'I cannot tell jokes because I do not understand them' (p.10), and gives the example of his father's joke: 'His face was drawn but the curtains were real' (p.10). This joke is a pun, which is a variety of ambiguity, since it plays on three different meanings of the word 'drawn'. Christopher finds this confusing because 'making the word mean the three different things at the same time...is like three people trying to talk to you at the same time about different things' (p.10).

Irony

Although he doesn't mention it specifically, Christopher doesn't like irony either, because irony depends on there being two possible meanings to a statement, a literal meaning and an ironic meaning. When Christopher asks the man in the shop near Willesden Junction whether the book he is looking at is the A to Z, the man replies, "No, it's a sodding crocodile" (p.229). This sarcastic answer is a form of irony, where what the man *really* means is 'of course it's the A to Z!' Christopher misses this irony, and asks the question again 'because it wasn't a crocodile and I thought I had heard wrongly because of his accent' (p.229).

Metaphor and Simile

Christopher explains that the second reason he finds people confusing is that 'people often talk using metaphors' (p.19). A metaphor 'is when you describe something by using a word for something that it isn't' (p.20). A metaphor like 'We had a real pig of a day', according to Christopher, 'should be called a lie because a pig is not like a day' (p.20).

On the other hand, Christopher frequently uses simile, which is a comparison between two things that literally are alike. He says the policeman's hairy nose 'looked as if there were two very small mice hiding in his nostrils' (p.22). In a footnote he explains that, because 'it really did look like there were two very small mice hiding in his nostrils', this makes it a simile, not a metaphor, and 'a simile is not a lie' (p.22).

Literary Language

Christopher's distrust of metaphors is one of the reasons why he doesn't like 'proper novels':

> In proper novels people say things like, 'I am veined with iron… I cannot contract into the firm fist which those clench who do not depend on stimulus.' What does this mean? I do not know (p.5).

Here, the author, Mark Haddon, is having a joke at the expense of 'purple prose', literary language that is excessively metaphorical. In a later chapter, Christopher discusses *The Hound of the Baskervilles* and says he doesn't like the part about the ancient scroll 'because it is written in old language which is difficult to understand' (p.89), and because Sir Arthur Conan Doyle uses metaphors such as 'some hardness, perhaps of eye' (p.90) which he finds confusing. On the other hand, Christopher says 'it's fun not knowing what the words mean because you can look them up in a dictionary' (p.90). In other words, Christopher's problems with language turn around the concepts of ambiguity and metaphor, rather than vocabulary. He shows this in his summary of the contents of the scroll, where he amusingly combines his own idiom, or way of speaking (indicated by such expressions as 'to do sex'), with the distinctive idioms of Doyle's text:

> Sir Hugo Baskerville...was a wild, profane and godless man. And he tried to do sex with a daughter of a yeoman, but she escaped and he chased her across the moor. And his friends, who were dare-devil roisterers, chased after him (p.88) .

Christopher's Expressiveness

Christopher's approach to language is starkly literal. He wants words always to have only one, unambiguous meaning. He also wants words to refer to definite things or concepts, such as 'stone' or 'dead', rather than fuzzy metaphorical concepts like 'stone dead' (p.19). And, most importantly, he wants statements always to be truthful, and not to be, like novels, 'lies about things which didn't happen' (p.25).

Puns, ambiguities, irony and metaphor are part of the expressive resources of language that are at the heart of any novel – including *The Curious Incident...*. Christopher's preference for unambiguous language would appear to be a major shortcoming in a writer. However, sometimes Christopher is capable of more sophisticated kinds of expression.

One example is Christopher's talent for analogy. Many of Christopher's digressions on scientific and mathematical topics seem at first irrelevant. But often Christopher uses these discussions as analogies to illustrate a point in relation to his narrative. For instance, his discussion of the population of frogs in the school pond shows by analogy his confidence that just because things are mysteries 'that doesn't mean there isn't an answer to them' (p.125). This discussion comes immediately after he reads the first of his mother's letters, and reflects his confidence that he will find an explanation for this mystery.

A second example of Christopher's expressiveness is his occasional use of longer sentences in which a string of phrases is joined together by conjunctions ('and', 'or', 'but', 'because'). These passages usually occur when he is experiencing 'information overload'. Their breathless, accelerating urgency very effectively illustrates the sense of being overwhelmed by 'too much information coming into my head' (p.8), like the loaves stacking up in the bread-slicing machine, another analogy which Christopher uses to illustrate this experience.

These examples show that, despite his condition, Christopher is capable of being an effective communicator. However, we should always remember that Christopher is a fictional character, and that a real Christopher Boone would not have written such a novel. Instead, we should think of the novel as an example of how imagination can help us put ourselves in someone else's shoes and try to understand what the world is like from their perspective.

QUESTIONS & ANSWERS

This section focuses on your analytical writing on the text, and gives you strategies for producing high-quality responses in your coursework and exam essays.

Essay Topics

1. 'Christopher Boone seems utterly unsuited to narrating a novel but turns out to be a rather wonderful narrator.' Discuss.
2. 'Christopher Boone has all the qualities of a good detective except one: he has no insight into other people's emotions. For this reason, he gets almost everything wrong.' Discuss.
3. '*The Curious Incident...* is not a genuine novel of growth and development because the protagonist proves to be incapable of change.' Discuss.
4. 'While Christopher wishes to give his story a tidy ending, this only reveals his blindness to the messy emotional lives of the people around him.' Discuss.
5. 'One of the ironies of the novel is that we come to sympathise with Christopher's parents in ways perhaps not intended by Christopher himself.' Discuss.
6. 'Although he tells Christopher a cruel lie, Christopher's father is the person who emerges as the hero of the novel.' Discuss.
7. "But that's not the way I am and there's nothing I can do to change that."

   '*The Curious Incident...* shows that all people are capable of change if they have a goal they really care about.' Discuss.
8. '*The Curious Incident...* shows that neither logical reasoning nor emotional impulse can alone serve as a basis for our actions.' Discuss.
9. 'The fact that we relate to Christopher as a character shows that the similarities between people are much greater than the differences.' Discuss.
10. '*The Curious Incident...* isn't a novel about disability. It shows that everyone has 'behavioural problems' and 'special needs'.' Discuss.
11. "All happy families resemble one another, but each unhappy family is unhappy in its own way" (Leo Tolstoy). Is this true of the family portrayed in *The Curious Incident...*?

12 'The way Christopher tells his story causes us to question our own commonsense perceptions and the erratic emotionalism of our lives.' Discuss.

Analysing a Sample Topic

7 "But that's not the way I am and there's nothing I can do to change that."

'*The Curious Incident*... shows that all people are capable of change if they have a goal they really care about.' Discuss.

Sample Approach to the Topic: Agreement with the Proposition

The essay topic contains three parts. The first is a quote from the novel, which you should recognise as coming from Christopher's mother's letter where she tries to explain why she left. The second is a more general proposition, or contention, making a claim about the novel as a whole that seems to contradict the first part. The third part, 'Discuss', asks you to consider both these statements together. Your essay should respond to the general proposition that the novel shows that people are capable of change. Indicate to what extent you agree with the statement, and *why*. Use evidence from the text to give examples of characters who change or who fail to change. In doing so, you should also discuss the quote from Christopher's mother, showing where it fits into the novel and how it relates to the main argument.

Note that the proposition applies to *all* people (which means you should discuss other characters as well as Christopher's mother), and it specifies 'if they have a goal they really care about'. You should discuss the importance of having a goal in this process of change.

Your opening paragraph might summarise the contradiction between the two statements, and sketch out your reasons for agreement with the contention, as in this example:

In *The Curious Incident*..., Christopher's mother writes to her son that she left partly because of the continual conflicts between her and Christopher and Christopher's father. She admits she is short-tempered and feels pessimistic about her power to change this. However, by the end of the novel she is making an effort to take control over her emotions: she sees a doctor and receives medication for depression, and attempts to be patient in dealing with Christopher. Similarly, Christopher's father vows to regain Christopher's trust by always being truthful, and Christopher, by making the journey to London, shows that he is able to overcome some aspects of his condition. Each of these characters tries to take control of their 'behavicural problems' in order to rebuild relationships that are important to them.

Your paragraphs could be organised in various ways. Here is one suggestion, focusing the main argument on the quote from Christopher's mother:

- Discuss the first quote. Where does it occur in the novel? What does Christopher's mother mean and why does she say this? Suggest reasons why she might feel pessimistic about her ability to cope with Christopher's problems.
- Discuss the second proposition in relation to Christopher's mother. Show how later events in the novel indicate that she attempts to change her behaviour, and identify the goals that inspire this change.
- Discuss the second proposition in relation to Christopher: how do his goals of discovering who killed Wellington and finding his mother inspire him to overcome his fears? Show what skills and knowledge Christopher learns, and how these change his outlook on life.
- Discuss the second proposition in relation to Christopher's father. Show how he has to face up to his mistakes, such as lying to Christopher and killing Wellington, and how he tries to make amends and rebuild his relationship with Christopher.

A sample conclusion:

In her letter, Christopher's mother seems pessimistic about her capacity to overcome the short-temperedness that strains her relationships. After a crisis in which she breaks up with Mr Shears, she returns to Swindon, seeks treatment for depression, and starts a new life. When she left her family she felt as if she wasn't needed, and receiving no response to her letters would have confirmed this. When she realises Christopher needs her support, she takes responsibility both for herself and for her son, signalling a positive outlook in dealing with her problems. So, too, Christopher learns to overcome his fears and take responsibility for some of his behaviour, while Christopher's father tries to make amends for his mistakes. Each of them has the goal of rebuilding an important relationship in their life and sets about achieving personal change to accomplish this.

Another Approach: Disagreement with the Proposition

You may feel that the novel is not as optimistic about the possibilities for personal change as the response above indicates. In disagreeing wholly with the main contention, you might argue that, whatever their personal goals and however they strive to change their behaviour, each character's basic nature remains the same. You might use evidence from the end of the novel to show that Christopher's mother is still prone to be emotional and short-tempered, Christopher's father is still the same patient and caring person he was at the beginning, and Christopher is still emotionally disconnected from his parents. You might argue that people can learn to get on better with each other, but this involves learning to compromise rather than changing who they are.

In partially disagreeing with the contention, you might argue that only some people are capable of change, or that all people are capable of change but only to a limited extent. For instance, you might argue that Christopher's mother and father try to learn from their mistakes, but this doesn't essentially change their characters. They will still have to confront the same problems of dealing with their emotions. You might also show that Christopher learns to overcome some of his fears and develop new confidence, but he doesn't make any progress in terms of feeling empathy for other people.

REFERENCES & READING

Text

Haddon, Mark, *The Curious Incident of the Dog in the Night-time*, David Fickling Books, Oxford, 2003.

Newspaper Articles and Author Interviews

Ezard, John, 'Curious incident of writer's literary hat trick', *Guardian*, 13 November 2003, http://www.guardian.co.uk/uk_news/story/0,3604,1083638,00.html

'Good questions, wicked answers', *Guardian*, 7 June 2003, http://books.guardian.co.uk/review/story/0,12084,971979,00.html

Haddon, Mark, 'Mark Haddon Q&A', *Guardian Unlimited* website, http://booktalk.guardian.co.uk/WebX?128@@.685ef53d

McInerney, Jay, 'The Remains of the Dog', *New York Times*, 15 June 2003, Section 7, p.5, http://query.nytimes.com/gst/fullpage.html?res=9905EED81E30F936A25755C0A9659C8B63

Schofield, William, 'A Journey to shock and enlighten', *Guardian*, 29 January 2004, http://books.guardian.co.uk/whitbread2003/story/0,14026,1135593,00.html

Shuttleworth, Mike, 'A Curious Bestseller', *The Age*, 14 February 2004, Review, p.3.

Walsh, John, 'This year's big read', *Independent*, 22 January 2004, p.2.

Other References

Abrams, M.H., *A Glossary of Literary Terms*, CBS Publishing, New York, 1981.

American Psychiatric Association, *Diagnostic and Statistical Manual of Mental Disorders: DSM-IV*, 4th edition, American Psychiatric Association, Washington, D.C., 1994.

Doyle, Arthur Conan, *The Adventures of Sherlock Holmes*, Wordsworth Editions, Ware, 1995.

Szatmari, Peter, 'Asperger's Disorder and Atypical Pervasive Developmental Disorder', in Fred R. Volkmar, ed., *Psychoses and Pervasive Developmental Disorders in Childhood and Adolescence*, American Psychiatric Press, Washington, D.C., 1996, pp.191-221.